Adult Analysis and Childhood Sexual Abuse

Adult Analysis and Childhood Sexual Abuse

edited by
Howard B. Levine

THE ANALYTIC PRESS

1990   Hillsdale, NJ   Hove and London

Published by The Analytic Press, Inc., Hillsdale, NJ.

Distributed solely by

Lawrence Erlbaum Associates, Inc., Publishers
365 Broadway
Hillsdale, New Jersey   07642

Library of Congress Cataloging-in-Publication Data

Adult analysis and childhood sexual abuse / edited by Howard B.
Levine
                    p.   cm.
    Includes bibliographical references.
    Includes indexes
    ISBN 0-88163-083-7
    1. Adult child sexual sexual abuse victims--Mental health.
    2. Psychotherapy. 3. Psychoanalysis. I. Levine, Howard B.
    [DNLM: 1. Child Abuse, Sexual--psychology.
    2. Incest--psychology. 3. Psychoanalysis.
    WM 460.5.S3 A244]
RC569.5.A28A33   1990
616.85'822--dc20
DNLM/DLC
for Library of Congress   0-780
                                                         CIP

Printed in United States of America
10 9 8 7 6 5 4 3 2 1

CONTENTS

CLINICAL CONSIDERATIONS
AND PSYCHOANALYTIC PROCESS

ISSUES OF TECHNIQUE

ACKNOWLEDGMENTS

Becoming a psychoanalyst requires as long and slow a passage as developing analytic understanding itself. If one is fortunate, it is a process that draws upon the many different relationships and experiences that one has in the course of one's life. Thus, there is a very long list of family, teachers, analysts, supervisors, colleagues, patients, and friends to whom I am deeply appreciative and indebted for the lifetime of help, support, instruction, and inspiration that they have provided in helping me to arrive at where I am today. Although my thanks to them is unending, their numbers require that they remain unnamed.

The preparation of this book was made immeasurable easier by a small group of colleagues and friends who worked together with me in the Workshop on the Analysis of Adults Who Were Sexually Abused as Children, held at the Boston Psychoanalytic Society and Institute from 1988–1990. Many of the ideas that appear under my own name and that informed my editorial activities were borrowed from, jointly developed with, or emerged in discussion with Drs. Susan Adelman, Enid Caldwell, Judith Huizenga, Mort Newman, and Ben Rubenstein. I would like to thank them for their acuity and generosity in sharing with me the richness of their clinical experience and wisdom.

I was also fortunate enough to have as contributors people who were dedicated, as clinicians, to their patients; as authors, to the rigors of analytic scholarship; and as colleagues, to the needs and well-being of their editor. I could not imagine an easier, more responsible, or more responsive group with whom to work. Similarly, my friends and colleagues at The Analytic Press, particularly Paul Stepansky and Eleanor Starke Kobrin, have provided occasional council and continued support that has been sustaining. For all of this, I am deeply grateful.

Last in printed order, but most cherished of all, is the love, encouragement, assistance, and patience of my family. For my wife, Susie, a special thank you for the childcare coverage and the uncomplaining way in which you took on my portion of so many domestic tasks that fell to you as I sat writing or reading. And for my son, Charlie, my love and thanks for allowing me to take time away from our time together and to use more than my share of the computer when I had to get the work out!

CONTRIBUTORS

Anne E. Bernstein, M.D., Clinical Professor of Psychiatry, Columbia University College of Physicians and Surgeons; Collaborating Psychoanalyst, Columbia University Psychoanalytic Center.

Julien Bigras, M.D. (deceased), Training and Supervising Analyst, Canadian Institute of Psychoanalysis; Member, Sociètè? Psychoanalytique de Montrèal.

J. Alexis Burland, M.D., Training and Supervising Analyst, Philadelpha Psychoanalytic Institute; Clinical Professor of Psychiatry and Human Behavior, Jefferson Medical College of Thomas Jefferson University, Philadelphia, PA.

Judith N. Huizinga, M.D., Faculty, Harvard University Medical School, Cambridge Hospital; Faculty, Boston Psychoanalytic Society and Institute

Selma Kramer, M.D., Professor of Psychiatry, Jefferson Medical College of Thomas Jefferson University, Philadelphia, PA; and Training and Supervising Analyst, Adult and Child Psychoanalysis, Philadelphia Psychoanalytic Institute.

Howard B. Levine, M.D. (editor), Faculty, Boston Psychoanalytic Institute; private practice of psychoanalysis.

Nydia Lisman-Pieczanski, M.D., Faculty Member, Buenos Aires Psychoanalytic Association; Associate Member, British Psycho-Analytical Society.

David L. Raphling, M.D., Training and Supervising Analyst, Washington Psychoanalytic Institute; Clinical Professor of Psychiatry, Uniformed Services University of the Health Sciences.

Raymond A. Raskin, M.D., Training and Supervising Analyst, Columbia University Psychoanalytic Center for Training and Research; Assistant Clinical Professor of Psychiatry, Columbia University College of Psyicians and Surgeons.

Susan P. Sherkow, M.D., Assistant Clinical Professor of Psychiatry, Albert Einstein College of Medicine: Qualified Child and Adolescent Analyst, New York Psychoanalytic Institute.

Brandt F. Steele, M.D., Professor of Psychiatry, Emeritus, University of Colorado Health Sciences Center; Consulting Psychiatrist, Kempe National Center for Prevention and Treatment of Child Abuse and Neglect, Denver, CO.

Adult Analysis and Childhood Sexual Abuse

Introduction
and
Overview

1

Introduction

Howard B. Levine

In recent years, the evaluation, treatment, and long-term consequences of childhood sexual trauma have occasioned increasing concern among mental health professionals. Surveys of randomly selected white middle-class or college-age women, by researchers such as Gagnon, Kinsey, Landis, and Finkelhor, have established that in these two subgroups, the incidence of potentially traumatic childhood sexual experience is approximately 20–33% (reported in Herman, 1981, pp. 12–13). These studies are problematic because the definitions of the event surveyed for—a "childhood sexual encounter with an adult male"—vary and are so broadly construed as to include such experiences as an encounter with an exhibitionist, which might more accurately be seen as unpleasant, but not necessarily pathogenic, when viewed over time in relation to ego development and character formation. They also fail to consider the possibility that the childhood sexual abuse occurred at the hands of an adult female (Kramer, 1983; and this volume), events that presumably would raise even higher the reported incidence of occurrence. In any case, even accepting these studies as reported, and correcting for potentially nontraumatic events, still leaves approximately 15% of the women surveyed who reported a childhood sexual encounter involving *physical contact* with an adult male.

In the same studies, 4% to 12% of the women surveyed reported a childhood "sexual experience with a relative" and 1% identified that relative as a father or stepfather. The incidence of reported childhood sexual encounters among adult males has not been as well studied as it has been for women, but the described range of occurrence varies from 8.5% to 30%. Thus, while it is true that a sexual *encounter* is not necessarily equivalent to a sexual *trauma*, the incidence of occurrence of the former is so high as to define a population at risk for potentially traumatic childhood sexual experiences, including incest with adult family members, that is considerable.

These figures were confirmed in anecdotal fashion when I first began to discuss the feasibility of this book with colleagues. While almost no one that I contacted had extensive experience with this group of patients—Drs. Bigras and Steele (this volume) were notable exceptions—most analysts reported having treated several adults who as children either had been involved in an incestuous relationship or had suffered a sexual trauma. A cursory search of the literature revealed a growing number of recent articles devoted to the subject of childhood sexual abuse, particularly in child, developmental, and forensic psychiatry and psychology journals. The analytic literature in this area, however, has barely begun to emerge. In particular, questions of technique and studies of the analytic process in adults who were sexually abused as children are yet to be thoroughly raised and examined.

This book is the attempt of a number of dedicated and experienced clinicians to remedy this oversight. Its scope is clinical. Its aim is to explore the problems of technique that are often encountered in attempts to treat these patients in psychoanalysis. As will quickly become apparent to the reader, we are dealing with a heterogeneous group of patients that defies simple categorization or generalization. And yet the various issues and challenges to technique that many of these patients present are similar enough to warrant their being studied as a group.

Before we begin, however, and by way of further introduction,

I would like to offer some thoughts on Freud's seduction hypothesis, the recent controversy that has come to surround it, and the nature and complexity of the trauma in childhood sexual abuse.

II

Beginning with Freud's (1896a,b) early attempts to understand the etiology of neurosis, psychoanalysts have long been interested in the impact of actual trauma on the evolution of symptoms and character traits. Recently, however, this subject became the center of controversy. Masson (1984) accused Freud of turning his back on the facts of actual traumatic childhood sexual experience when Freud abandoned his original hypothesis of the role of seduction in the etiology of neurosis for a formulation of neurosogenesis that emphasized, instead, fantasy, psychic reality, and the psychological derivatives of developmentally determined infantile sexuality. While I do not share Masson's position, I do feel that in making the necessary and useful shift away from the seduction hypothesis toward a more complex theory that encompasses psychic reality and the vicissitudes of fantasies related to infantile sexual and aggressive wishes, Freud inadvertently may have contributed to a tendency in psychoanalysis to downplay the impact of actual traumatic events on the etiology of neurosis. In retrospect, one might imagine that this tendency was abetted by the fascination that the newly discovered intrapsychic domain held for those working within the young field of psychoanalysis and by the need of analysts continually to emphasize and demonstrate to a skeptical and resistant audience of critics the power and effect of unconscious, subjective, infantile forces operating within the psyche.

While a full-ranging exploration of these important issues would take us too far afield, they are certainly relevant referents for the readers of this book. They form a very complicated chapter in the history of the evolution of psychoanalytic thought and are related to many important issues that are currently being debated in psychoanalytic discourse. These include whether psychoanalysis is a natural scientific or hermeneutic discipline; the value and meaning of reconstruction; the truth status of the data generated in the psychoanalytic encounter; and the relationship between narrative truth and psychic reality on one hand and historical truth and objective reality on the other. For now, however, because Freud's attitude toward the place of actual childhood seduction and his reasons for abandoning the seduction hypothesis have been so misunderstood recently, and because these issues form such an important historical backdrop to the clinical issues with which we are concerned, I thought it would be worthwhile to spend a bit of time examining them.

Freud (1896a,b) originally concluded that an *actual seduction* taking place prior to puberty was at the etiological root of the neuroses. He believed that the affects and memories linked to that experience were disavowed and sequestered in the child's psyche until they were reawakened by the normal developmental processes of adolescence, with their inevitable stirring of sexual feelings. It was only then that the childhood experience became dynamically activated as a trauma. To quote Freud (1896a), ". . . it is not the experiences themselves which act traumatically but their revival as a *memory* after the subject has entered on sexual maturity" (p. 164). The result was felt to be a form of psychic economic imbalance that gave rise to conflict, repression, and the development of neurotic symptoms.

An immediate problem we encounter in evaluating this formulation today is that it is inextricably linked with a model of mental functioning that, while ingenious as a first formulation, is overly simplistic compared with our current models of the mind and therefore is no longer tenable. This is not to say that childhood trauma does not cause dissociative reactions in the mind of the developing child or that some symptomatic outbreaks may not occur only after becoming psychically activated by later events, such as the onset of puberty—they do. But far more goes into the experiencing and processing of actual events and into the complex forces that eventuate in pathogenesis than this first model allows.

A second, even more important, objection is that we do not have adequate access to the data base on which Freud formulated his seduction hypothesis. Most notably, we do not know to what extent he *reconstructed* the childhood sexual seductions from less direct material presented to him by his patients. That is, were his patients *reporting* that such and such had happened, or was it Freud's *interpretation* that such and such must have happened, based on his sense of the unconscious meaning of the patient's dreams, associations, and behavior within the analytic sessions? To the extent to which the latter may be the case, this does not necessarily invalidate the historical accuracy of Freud's reconstructions. It does, however, make it quite difficult for us to evaluate the evidentiary basis on which Freud's seduction theory was constructed. (Schimek (1987) reviews this subject in detail and concludes that Freud's evidence was mainly, although not exclusively, derived from reconstruction rather than direct patient report.)

The picture is further complicated by the fact that Freud developed the seduction theory before he had formulated the concept of transference as we know it today. His technique at the time was imbued with a stance that was forceful, positive, and determined. It was not long before that he had abandoned the "pressure technique"—pressing on a patient's forehead in an attempt to stimulate thoughts and memories—for a verbal insistance that something must be coming to mind. His method still attempted to circumvent resistances rather than analyze them. He would not take no for an answer. In the light of our current sensitivity to the impact of the analyst's actual behavior on the development of the transference neurosis (Gill, 1982), we can only imagine how this must have been experienced by Freud's patients and the kinds of fantasies that it stimulated. Even more to the point, Freud's forceful, albeit well-intended, intrusions into the inner life of his patients must have been quite stimulating and frightening to those analysands who had experienced actual childhood seductions or sexual traumata. From the perspective of our current knowledge, it would not be too far afield to surmise that such forceful intrusions were, in at least some instances, countertransference enactments in which a childhood sexual trauma was symbolically being repeated. Thus, it remains quite unclear how much Freud's reconstructions were based on observations of what we would now view as erotized transference phenomena, how often these transferences reflected childhood fantasies as opposed to actual childhood seductions or sexual trauma, or the extent to which Freud recognized the possibility that his analysands' transferences may have colored their reports of earlier childhood events.

As will become abundantly clear in the chapters that follow, the experience of a childhood sexual seduction can have a significant impact on a patient's subsequent behavior and transference, lending them a strong erotic cast. The presence of a sexualized transference by no means excludes the possibility of a childhood sexual trauma. In some instances, it may even be a presumptive indicator that such a trauma has occurred. My point, however, is that *we are unable to accurately evaluate the nature and basis for Freud's evidence in formulating the seduction hypothesis.* Thus, the possibility exists that the still nascent stage of the analytic theory and technique on which he had to depend left Freud with a methodology that was not adequate to the task of discerning actual from fantasied childhood traumata and that he was led to his conclusions in part by his theoretical preconceptions of what he would find, rather than by the data of his clinical encounters.

As for Freud himself, although his theory and practice of analytic technique underwent many productive changes as he vigorously pursued the implications of psychic reality and fantasy formation, he never lost sight of the fact that some patients had, indeed, experienced childhood sexual trauma. His formulation of the basis for the Wolf Man's neurosis (Freud, 1918), as well as numerous first-hand accounts of analyses with Freud (see Ruitenbeek, 1973), indicates the extent to which Freud continued to rely on reconstruction of what he believed to be actual events. Throughout his career, Freud remained convinced of the impact of real traumatic events, including sexual traumata, on the lives of his patients. As noted by Bernstein (this volume), subsequent to giving up the seduction hypothesis, Freud made several observations that reflected his recognition that his patients' tales of childhood seduction have not been mere fantasy. For example: "Phantasies of being seduced are of particular interest because so often they are not phantasies but real memories" (Freud, 1917, p. 370); "Actual seduction is common enough" (Freud, 1931, p. 232). "The object of sexual seduction may direct her later sexual life so as to provoke entirely similar acts" (Freud, 1939, pp. 75–76). Or, "The childhood experiences constructed or remembered in analysis are sometimes indisputably false and sometimes equally certainly correct, and in most cases compounded of truth and falsehood" (Freud, 1917, p. 367).

And, of course, despite the general tendency in psychoanalysis to scrutinize any reported memory for reflected, conflict-derived meanings and for important implications for and derivations from the current transference dispositions, many analysts have continued to recognize and write about the meaning and importance of actual trauma, including childhood sexual seduction. Here, I would just like to mention in passing—and pay special tribute to—Phyllis Greenacre, who has made many outstanding contributions to the analytic literature in this regard. For example, in her 1956 paper, "Re-Evaluation of the Process of Working Through," she wrote,

> we know, but often forget, that specific "fantasies" which persist until adult life are rarely *only* "typical" fantasies, common to all infantile development, but rather those typical ones which have been given a special strength, form and pressure for repetition through having been confirmed by external events [p. 643]

Greenacre's view takes into account that a child's subjective experience will be heavily determined by the instinctual conflicts and developmental issues with which he or she is currently struggling. Thus, a child grappling with issues of autonomy or control of aggression will tend to experience affectively important events along these lines. Similarly, an oedipal-aged or fixated child will experience affectively important events in terms of rivalry, conquest, castration threats, and the like. This is not to say that the actual, objective form and content of the experience will not lend their particular stamp to the way in which the event is experienced. Rather, the child's subjective experience of the event—its psychic reality—will be codetermined by the quality and nature of the actual event and the intrapsychic state of the mind in which that event occurs.

The issue is even more complicated, because as Greenacre

(1950, 1956) also notes, a child may unconsciously seek to initiate a particular kind of traumatic experience in the complex service of repetition and attempted mastery. Thus, the line between psychic reality (i.e., unconsciously determined perception) and objective reality (i.e., historical fact) is never quite free from potential unconscious influence.

III

Given the many advances in our views since 1896, how, then, do we now understand the immediate impact of childhood trauma on the development of the psyche? Unlike Freud, whose first formulations were made in the absence of child analytic data, we are far more sensitized to the existence of the direct consequences of childhood sexual trauma and aware of the complex ways in which very young children experience, adapt to, remember, and transform their memories of the significant events in their lives. (See for example Kris, 1956). And while the matter of delayed action as a mechanism in symptom formation is still very much a part of analytic thinking, we no longer rely on it as the sole explanation for understanding the long-term consequences of early childhood traumata.

A more contemporary view of the impact of a sexual—or any other—trauma on a child, considers the way in which that trauma is experienced in line with current developmental conflicts and issues and how it is responded to by the child and his or her network of supportive objects. Our focus includes an appreciation of how the trauma became elaborated in fantasy and play, connected with character formation and symptoms (including the regressive reversal of previously obtained levels of development), and contributed to subsequent developmental disturbances; and how the affects and memory traces connected to the trauma underwent repression, distortion, and symbolic elaboration.

This thinking is reflected in more contemporary definitions of sexual abuse, such as that offered by Brandt Steele (this volume). Steele defines sexual abuse as

the involvement of dependent, developmentally immature children in sexual activity that they do not fully comprehend, without consideration for their stage of psychosocial sexual development. [This involvement can occur in many forms and] at any age from infancy through adolescence with various family members, relatives or strangers. It can be a single, isolated incident or repeated frequently over many years. It may be homosexual or heterosexual with either girls or boys and involve anything from fondling to full genital intercourse or variations of oral and anal contact. It may be done with some degree of love and gentleness or involve verbal threats and physical violence. All these variables have a bearing on what the sexual experience means to the child and how it is woven into the child's psychic development and affects later behavior. . . . [T]he sexual events themselves are not the simple, direct cause of subsequent difficulties. . . . The trouble comes when the sexual activities are instigated by a person older than the child and are beyond the child's ability to truly understand or emotionally manage the affects and conflicts that are generated. The activity is not a consensual one between peers but is exploitative, more for the satisfaction of the perpetrator than of the child victim. . . . [T]he degree of trauma is related to the discrepancy between the intensity of the noxious stimulae and the ability of the child's ego to cope.

In short, quoting again from Steele (1981), *"The essence of the abusive element in the sexual activity is the misuse of the immature child by the adult for the solving of problems and satisfying of adult needs, while disregarding the appropriate needs and developmental state of the child."* (p. 233, italics added).

A recent article by Galenson (submitted) illustrates the profound impact of a single sexual trauma on a two-and-a-half-year-old girl named Jenny, who had had a reasonably good pre-traumatic adjustment. The richness and relevance of Galenson's case report makes it a unique contribution to the literature, one worth considering in detail.

One day, while watching her parents undress, Jenny pointed to her mother's genitals and said that the neighbor's boy, Sam, had "a toy in his tush." This statement and her increasing mood disturbance, irritability, and emerging sleep disturbance had caused the parents considerable uneasiness, and they began to review the events of the prior two weeks in some detail. They remembered that several weeks ago, Jenny had spent the evening with her next door neighbors, where the sitter for the evening was their 15-year-old son. In retrospect, the parents now realized that a number of the changes in Jenny dated to that time. She had begun to stay away from other children and she avoided her formerly beloved puzzles and blocks which she now called "sticky and goofy." Furthermore, while she had not been particularly interested in doll play previously, there had been a sudden upsurge in her interest in dolls. She also demanded a drink of water whenever she became upset, and this hitherto casually clean child now washed her hands repeatedly at every opportunity.

In addition to these changes in her general behavior and in her play, her relationship with her mother had also changed. She was often angry at her mother, and she expressed this largely in trying to bite and kick at her mother's breasts. Finally, a major regression to orality in various forms had begun to characterize this formerly self-sufficient little girl. She now demanded her bottles, which she drank during the day as well as at night, and refused most solid foods, in contrast to her former hearty appetite for salads and her only occasional use of the bottle.

Those symptoms and changes led Jenny's parents to question the neighbor's son about his babysitting experience with her. He acknowledged having allowed Jenny into the bathroom with him while he urinated, something that Jenny was used to doing with her own parents, but denied that anything unusual had taken place. Still concerned about Jenny's behavior, her parents then consulted Galenson, who

saw Jenny together with her mother in a play interview. The dainty, pretty little girl came in readily but did not seem particularly pleased with the toys in the room. She immediately asked that [Galenson] place one of the dolls on the small potty chair in the playroom, spread the doll's legs apart, and then undressed and examined all the other dolls in the playroom in turn. She then asked for a drink of water and drank several cups in succession, saying that she was thirsty but giving no further explanation. She refused to touch any of the puzzles in the playroom but began to play with the blocks, which she piled in a tall tower and left them standing intact. Turning to the crayons, she was extremely distressed to find a broken yellow crayon, refused to touch this one or to touch any of the others which were intact. She then went to the sink, where she washed her hands a number of times and asked [Galenson] to take her to the bathroom where she urinated. [Thus ended the] first play session . . . and she left in a somewhat lighter mood.

Galenson notes that

much of the behavior which had been described . . . by her parents during [their] initial interview appeared during this play session. . . . Her interest in genitals was apparent, her mood was fairly somber; she avoided playing with puzzles and washed her hands and was very thirsty. Her building with blocks was unusual in that she created a phallic-shaped structure which she insisted on leaving in its place. Her thirst seemed directly connected with the hand washing, and with the urination which followed. I concluded from this first interview that there was undue concern about the genital difference, a concern which was in some way connected with the oral behavior reflected in her excessive thirst. It was evident that Jenny was repeating in her play an experience which had included the use of her mouth combined with genital awareness or stimulation, behaviors suggesting that there had been some form of contact between Jenny's mouth and Sam's penis and his urination as well.

Jenny's father attempted to treat her himself in the fashion of the Little Hans case. He kept a careful diary and consulted with Dr. Galenson along the way. The notes in the diary in the week following the consultation offered the following:

On returning home from their interview . . . the parents remembered that Jenny's nose had begun to run constantly during the preceding few weeks, a symptom which they had attributed to a mild upper respiratory infection. Now they suspected that this symptom was connected in some way with her traumatic experience since there were no other accompanying respiratory symptoms. The running nose suggested to the parents that engorgement of the nasal mucosa may have taken place in this child much as adult females experience nasal engorgement during sexual arousal.

According to the father's notes, Jenny suggested during their first play session together that they play the game "bounce," a game which she had often played with her friends. She indicated that they were to sit on the edge of her bed and bump their buttocks up and down. This was clearly a masturbatory game which apparently had gone on for some time in the past. Jenny next lay down on her bed, opened her mouth and pretended that she was choking, after which she said to her father, "It burns, get me water." She then drank the water he brought her, complained that her stomach hurt, and then went to her blocks. She said that green was her color and yellow was her daddy's, and immediately asked that she be able to watch her father urinate in the bathroom. Her father avoided doing this, and instead Jenny then went on to place two red blocks on the surface of each of her thighs as she sat on the floor. . . .

During the night following this first therapeutic interview with her father, Jenny awoke and told her father about several experiences she remembered, all of which had involved him in some way during the prior year. These included being in a swimming pool with him, watching him leave on a trip by airplane for the first time, and some fear of one of her puzzles which her father had brought home as a gift. All of these incidents appeared, in retrospect, to have been connected with anxiety over loss. In the pool incident, the loss of body boundaries, object loss in relation to her father's departure on the plane, and fear of bodily disintegration as she watched pieces of the puzzle fall apart. [In the light of this data, Galenson] thought it likely that Jenny had indeed experienced a traumatic confrontation with Sam, in which some contact with his urinating penis had intensified her dawning age-appropriate awareness and concern about the genital difference, which had begun to emerge before the event had occurred. It seemed clear that her fears of body dissolution and object loss were now revived again. . . .

As the father continued to record the events of Jenny's life, there were many references to her biting and to her preoccupation with broken things during the next few days. For example, she bit the trunk of a toy elephant as well as protuberances in other toy animals, and once again she pointed to many broken objects as she had previously done during her 19th and 20th months, before the traumatic event. These "broken objects" included the half-moon in the sky at night. She now began to accuse her father of having broken her crayons and she became anxious in his presence, sitting with her back turned to him as if to protect herself from him. [Galenson understood these latter symptoms as] a revival of her pre-oedipal castration fears, and the wish to have her father's penis by biting it off. . . .

At the end of the first week, Jenny complained that her bicycle seat and her chair were sticky, and she began to take off her underpants, complaining they were "hot." She no longer spoke about growing up to be a lady as she had before the traumatic event, and instead retreated into ever more babyish ways. As her father sat near her bed one evening she told him "a man came into my mouth," and then she complained that her nose itched.

Material of this latter sort led Dr. Galenson to conclude that "fellatio had been attempted as part of the traumatic event."

In a second consultative session occurring two weeks after the first,

Jenny proceeded to undress all the dolls completely, remarking on their hair, shoes and a red hair-bow worn by one of the dolls. During this play she asked for water to drink constantly as she did at home, and explained . . . that her mouth was "hot." Then she pointed to the various male–female differences between each of the dolls, ultimately including the explicitly genital differences as the session came to a close.

The play during this session was intense and much more complex than it had been previously. It was focused to begin with on the genital displacements from genitals to hair, shoes and then hair-bow, all connected with the central issue of the genital difference. The "hot" sensation was now displaced upward to her mouth from her former "hot" underpants, representing, as she attempted to deal in a number of ways, with the discomfort of her genital arousal.

Subsequently, Galenson offered the following short term results of her intervention:

Although this child had regressed in many areas—her sleep disturbance, a disruption in her toilet training which had occurred, her serious anorexia and her regression to bottle feeding—she slowly began to improve. Her thirst diminished, she again began to speak of becoming a lady some day, and she gradually regained her former ability and interest in taking care of her own body and her own needs.

And some longer term follow-up:

[When Jenny was three, the birth of a sister produced] a definite regression in almost all major areas of functioning for a short period. [Her recovery was marked by] a definite increase in her moodiness and a tendency toward a general compliance which now consistently characterized her and was in contrast with her prior ebullience and independence. She also developed a number of rituals, including her insistence that all doors be tightly shut and that broken objects be discarded or avoided altogether.

[As Jenny grew, she] continued to be a compliant and somewhat moody child, in marked contrast to her early vivacity and curiosity which had been characteristic of her prior to the traumatic experience. It is difficult to say whether these changes can be attributed to the single traumatic experience, even if one takes into account the fact that she was at that time in the midst of an important phase of sexual development, the early genital phase. . . .

By the time Jenny had reached her early 20's, she was a talented young woman with many interests and very satisfactory academic attainments. However, she was somewhat disturbed by the fact that she suffered from a variety of fears and there were important inhibitions in regard to her heterosexual life.

This extended case report illustrates the enormous difficulty of fully understanding the impact of a single traumatic sexual event experienced by a preoedipal girl at the hands of a nonfamily member. It raises questions about actual and potential strengths and liabilities related to pre- and posttraumatic events and indicates the complexity of trying to isolate a single traumatic factor in development and follow its consequences through to outcomes in later life.

On the other hand, the evidence for the immediate traumatic impact of the seduction is compelling. We see the development of anxiety and conflict with a resort to repression, denial, displacement, somatization, and regression. There is symptom formation, impact on character structure and basic mood, consequences for her resiliency to deal with future stresses such as the birth of a sibling, and probable long-term implications for her development and adaptive ego capacity. Regressive manifestations include the resurgence of issues around recently mastered conflicts related to castration shock and the recognition of the anatomical sex difference. In addition, an important *advance* in development, the evolution of a capacity for complex symbolic expression, was probably precipitated by the sexual trauma, as evidenced by her new-found interest in and use of doll play.

Faced with the terrible complexity of this single sexual trauma, imagine how one might fare in an attempt to reconstruct and deal with its diverse manifestations and consequences 20 or 30 years later, when Jenny might present as an adult patient with such symptoms as depression, anxiety, phobias, compulsive traits, a sexual disturbance, or difficulties getting close to men. Or, how much more traumatic and complex the problems facing the adult patient and his or her analyst might be when that patient was repeatedly sexually traumatized in childhood or involved in an incestuous relationship with a primary parental object. And yet, these are the tasks that more and more of our patients present us in our clinical work.

IV

Steele (chapter 2) and Burland and Raskin (chapter 3) offer overviews that attempt to examine some of the adult consequences of childhood sexual abuse. Raphling (chapter 4) follows with a discussion of problems encountered in therapeutic alliance formation and the opening phase. Next, Bernstein (chapter 5), Sherkow (chapter 6), and Huizenga (chapter 7) present further case material illustrating problems in ego development specifically related to a childhood sexual trauma. Bernstein's cases describe a number of ego developmental issues, with a particular emphasis on their implications for the transference and countertransference. Sherkow's cases contrast the ego difficulties of an adult patient with those encountered in two children she had treated. Huizenga focuses on her patient's dream life and the ways in which dreams were used in the analysis to examine the development of symbolism, fantasy, and play, each of which had been constricted as a result of the childhood sexual trauma of paternal incest. Lisman-Pieczanski (chapter 8) presents a case analyzed from a Kleinian point of view, with a special emphasis on the countertransferences that were stimulated; and Kramer (chapter 9) discusses adult sexual dysfunction and learning disabilities as residues of childhood sexual traumata, a phenomenon that she calls "somatic memory." In the concluding section, "Issues of Technique," Bigras (chapter 10) and Levine (chapter 11) present broad discussions of clinical problems and issues of technique in the analysis of adults who were sexually abused as children.

As with any psychoanalytic exploration, we hope that our investigations will raise many more questions in the minds of our readers than we were able to answer. To do so, and to engage the interest and attention of analysts and other clinicians in continuing to examine the many important issues related to the analysis of adults who were sexually abused as children, is to fulfill the aim with which we began this work. We hope that our readers will agree that it was a worthwhile endeavor.

REFERENCES

Freud, S. (1896a), Further remarks on the neuropsychoses of defense. *Standard Edition*, 3:157–185. London: Hogarth Press, 1962.

_____ (1896b), The aetiology of hysteria. *Standard Edition*, 3:191–221. London, Hogarth Press, 1962.

_____ (1917), Introductory Lectures on Psychoanalysis. *Standard Edition*, 15 and 16. London: Hogarth Press, 1963.

_____ (1918), From the history of an infantile neurosis. *Standard Edition*, 17:1–122. London: Hogarth Press, 1957.

_____ (1931), Female sexuality. Standard Edition, 21:221–243. London: Hogarth Press, 1961.

_____ (1939), Moses and monotheism. *Standard Edition*, 22:3–127. London: Hogarth Press, 1964.

Galenson, E. (submitted), The capacity for fantasy and symbolic elaboration in a two and one half year old girl.

Gill, M. (1982), *Analysis of Transference. Vol. 1.* New York: International Universities Press.

Greenacre, P. (1950), The prepuberty trauma in girls. *Psychoanal. Quart.*, 19:298–317.

_____ (1956), Re-evaluation of the process of working through. In: *Emotional Growth*. New York: International Universities Press, 1971, pp. 641–650.

Herman, J. (1981), *Father-Daughter Incest*. Cambridge, MA: Harvard University Press.

Kramer, S. (1983), Object-coercive doubting: A pathological defensive response to maternal incest. *J. Amer. Psychoanal. Assn.*, Suppl. 31:325–351.

Kris, E. (1956), The recovery of childhood memories. The *Psychoanalytic Study of the Child* 11:54–88. New York: International Universities Press.

Masson, J. M. (1984), *The Assault on Truth*. New York: Farrar, Strauss, Giroux.

Ruitenbeek, H. M., ed. (1973), *Freud As We Knew Him*. Detroit, MI: Wayne State University Press.

Schimek, J. G. (1987), Fact and fantasy in the seduction theory: a historical review. *J. Amer. Psychoanal. Assn.* 35:937–966.

Steele, B. (1981), Long-term effects of sexual abuse in childhood. In: *Sexually Abused Children and Their Families*, ed. P. Mrazek & C. Kempe. New York: Pergamon Press, pp. 223–234.

2 Some Sequelae of the Sexual Maltreatment of Children

Brandt F. Steele

We define sexual maltreatment as the involvement of dependent, developmentally immature children in sexual activity that they do not fully comprehend and without consideration for their stage of psychosocial sexual development. Sexual abuse of children occurs in many varieties and can happen at any age from infancy through adolescence with various family members, relatives, or strangers. It can be a single, isolated incident or repeated frequently over many years. It may be homosexual or heterosexual with either girls or boys and involve anything from fondling to full genital intercourse or variations of oral and anal contact. It may be done with some degree of love and gentleness or involve verbal threats and physical violence.

All these variables bear on what the sexual experience means to the child and how it is woven into the child's psychic development and affects later behavior (Steele and Alexander, 1981). Yet the sexual events themselves are not the only, simple, direct cause of subsequent difficulties. Nearly all people, in their early lives, have had stimulating sexual contacts ranging from the curiosity-driven exploratory actions of little boys and girls in preschool years to the tentative, but more definitive, trial activities of pubertal children and adolescents in their dating activities. Such mutually agreeable sexual contacts seem to be educational and growth promoting rather than traumatic, especially if they are not harshly punished or dealt with by tales of frightful consequences.

The trouble comes when the sexual activities are instigated by a person older than the child and are beyond the child's ability to understand or emotionally manage the affects and conflicts that are generated. This kind of activity is not consensual between peers but, rather, is exploitative, more for the satisfaction of the perpetrator than the child victim. The more dominance and violence the perpetrator expresses, as in the extreme situation of rape, the more obvious is this exploitation and disregard. Yet, even in rape, the devastating consequences seem due more to the violence of the perpetrator and the relative helplessness of the victim than simply to the sexual aspects of the attack itself. Even in "milder" cases of sexual abuse, that is, where elements of violence, force, or cruel disregard for the feelings of the child are less prominent, the degree of trauma is related to the discrepancy between the intensity of the noxious stimulae and the ability of the child's ego to cope. The sexual experiences do not occur as isolated events in a neutral, standard background, but in a total context of the child's psychological development and the variable, complex family interaction. The preexisting family experience has a potent bearing on how the child can cope with the abusive episode. The quality of the relationships existing between the child and its caregivers and with the molester are as important as the sexual act itself—even more important—in the development of residual problems. Children may be especially vulnerable to such abuse if they have felt lonely and deprived of adequate care at home; they are receptive to interest and affection offered by others.

Children can feel damaged and betrayed by the pedophilic behavior not only of family caregivers but of such other trusted adults as teachers, scout masters, camp counselors, daycare providers. Self-image and reality perception can be further distorted if the child, reporting the events and seeking help, is disbelieved or accused of instigating the abuse.

Sexual molestation by outsiders in the form of exhibitionism and voyeurism, or the more serious actions of touching, grabbing, and fondling, in playgrounds, school corridors, and movie theaters may not be harmful to a child living in a normal, healthy

family. The child can report the incident to parents, be comforted and supported for the sense of hurt and outraged innocence, and helped to learn self-protective measures. Even
though there may be some distressing fear of strangers for a time,
the child still feels safe and loved at home. Self-protective ego
functions, aided by the auxiliary egos of the loving family,
prevent significant trauma. On the other hand, such happenings
can be traumatic if met with parental disbelief and accusations
that the child has a trouble-making imagination or has somehow
brought the trouble on himself. Lacking necessary empathic
support, children feel disturbingly overwhelmed, confused,
alone, and isolated even in their own home. At such times, the
defenses of denial, repression, or dissociation may be mobilized
with more or less success.

Abuse perpetrated by family members or family friends tends
to be more damaging than that instigated by strangers. It
involves betrayal and exploitation of the child by those older
caregivers and authorities to whom the child is attached and
obliged to trust. Those to whom the child would normally turn
for comfort and protection become those who hurt. The intrafamilial perpetrators of sexual acts with their children or younger
siblings typically demand secrecy, telling their victims that
these activities are special secrets between themselves and must
never be shared with others. Often the admonition to be silent is
coupled with bribes or threats of punishment or even of death if
the child tells. Thus, the child is further blocked in seeking help,
increasing the feeling of helplessness, aloneness, and distrust.

Seldom are intrafamilial sexual molestations entirely new
events occurring in previously well-functioning family systems.
The child is already programmed to be at risk and vulnerable to
abuse and its consequences. Often the parents are in a mutually
overly dependent and equally mutually unsatisfying relationship. In cases of significant sibling incest, it is common for one
or both parents to be involved in extramarital affairs or, if not
involved in such open marital breakdown, at least unable to give
adequate love and care to the children. Son and daughter feel
bereft and turn to each other for the love and affection not
available from parents. Both feel some reward in the relationship, but eventually the younger one, usually but not always the

girl, tends to feel betrayed and used, again with no place to go for comfort. Sometimes sexual abuse by an older person has preceded sibling incest.

In cases of parent–child incest, it is common for one or both parents to feel insufficiently understood and cared for by the other, resulting in unilateral or mutual withdrawal and lack of warm, loving interaction. The child inevitably feels uncared for, particularly by the parent who is more depressed, withdrawn, or uncaring. The other parent and the child, equally deprived and needy, turn to each other for care and affection, which easily becomes sexualized in a physical way. The child's libidinal attachment to the primary caregiver, and the child's expected cooperation with parental requests, are taken advantage of and exploited by the parent who fills a parental need without appropriate regard for the child's needs or limited understanding. There is further betrayal in the adult's misuse of the child's normal pleasure from stimulation of the erotic zones (e.g., "Do you want me to make it feel good down there?"). The child's search for pleasure and need satisfaction becomes inextricably linked with feeling exploited and disregarded, resulting in a life-long tendency to have difficulty in seeking pleasure, an inability to really enjoy pleasure, and an attachment to abusive love objects.

There are also highly patriarchal families in which wives and children are cowed into helpless submission and are sexually misused by older males as well as father. Physical violence may accompany the sexual demands. The devastating impact of sexual abuse in a Victorian patriarchal family is poignantly described in a recent biography of Virginia Woolf (De Salvo, 1989). Her experiences of being sexually abused by older half-brothers, dominated, disregarded, and emotionally abused by her father, and unaided by her overworked, helpless mother led to the low self-esteem, depression, and disturbed interpersonal relationships that haunted her for the rest of her life. Many of her writings about children and adolescents are fictionalized accounts of her own tragic life.

Inevitably, one is interested in understanding sexual abuse of children in the framework of the Oedipus complex, particularly in cases of intrafamilial incest. Following Waelder's (1960) description of the Oedipus complex as "a kind of premature rehearsal of the future sexual role with parents or parent substitutes as object, and with details varying with the child's environment" (p. 114), it is easy to see how distorted the child's Oedipus complex can be. Classically, a child has fantasies about genital sexual activities with the parent of opposite sex like those he believes the adults perform, along with fantasies of consequences of the act, and then relinquishes the fantasies because of their impracticality and ensuing guilt. In the sexual-abuse-prone family, no warm, libidinally satisfying parental relationship exists as a model to follow in fantasy. The child has already felt some degree of deprivation and approaches the "rehearsal of the future sexual role" with genital strivings much diluted by persistent yearnings for love and care on a dependent, infantile, preoedipal level. An ordinary, "healthy" Oedipus complex cannot develop under these circumstances. The boy can hardly turn with warm genital strivings to a cold, unempathic mother; the girl looks to father for basic maternal care. The child's neediness creates a vulnerability to any offers of love and care, and these can be channeled by the older person into premature sexual activity before the child is developmentally able to understand and integrate the experience.

Boys and girls alike may turn to fathers, other adults, or older siblings with largely unconscious longings to find a substitute for the early empathic care they lack. The girl has little fear of losing her mother's love because she has never felt she had it anyway. Neither boy nor girl seems greatly worried by competition with the same sex parent, since the parent has not shown a close relationship that could be significantly interfered with. In fact, parents often give the child the impression that their own relationship is unsatisfactory and that they are looking elsewhere for something. Further, parents often give tacit approval or even open encouragement to incestuous behaviors, despite professing ignorance of the situation. Superego formation, as it involves identification with parents, is inevitably distorted in such situations, and development of the ego function of knowing and utilizing reality is also disturbed. There is confusion about what is right and wrong. The incest is encouraged, approved, or even requested by a parent; yet the child is told that it is not to be spoken of lest there be trouble or punishment. The child also learns that society considers incest to be the ultimate in immorality. A child who does tell and is then accused of lying or imagining becomes puzzled about what is reality. Is one's own perception and inner reality true, or is the outer world telling the truth? There is self-doubt about one's own perceptions. There also seems confusion over the equivalence of sexual activity and loving care, the idea that sex is the primary, or only, pathway to giving or receiving love.

Such oedipal distortions persist and are seldom adequately reworked or resolved in adolescence. Various degrees of self-doubt, low self-esteem, unsureness of sexual identity, puzzlement about normal sexual roles, distrust of adults, helplessness or defensive aggressiveness, and excessive dependence tend to persist through adolescence and into adult life. Inevitably, relationships in dating, courtship, and marriage are disturbed to some extent, ranging from lonely avoidance and isolation to excessively active, tumultuous, short-lived, sadomasochistic alliances. Fortunately, many victims who were not seriously damaged and had periods of better empathic care can manage to suppress enough of their traumatic residues to lead at least superficially normal lives despite deeper levels of unhappiness.

Promiscuity in adolescence and later life is a common sequel to earlier incest, sex being thought of as the basic way to express love. Often a child is given special favors, privileges, or extra attention for providing sex to the adult and thus is led to consider and use sex as a commodity for trading or merchandising. Prostitution beginning in adolescence may be an expression of this concept. In prostitution, male victims of previous sex abuse tend to be exclusively homosexual, either active or passive, but may be bisexual in their personal lives. Sexual acts of pedophiles almost always begin in adolescence and can be either homosexual or heterosexual without direct relationship to previous abuse by males or females, although pedophilia is most commonly related to abuse by males early in life. Recently the sexual abuse of young children by older children has been reported (Cantwell, 1988; Johnson, 1989). The perpetrators ranged in age from 4 to 14 and were previously sexually abused themselves. The transition from victim to victimizer has not been adequately studied or understood. Litin, Griffin, and Johnson (1956) noted, "Such a child has no choice but to introject the confusion, guilt, fear of detection, anxiety, hostility, *and sanction* which it has just observed in the parents" (p. 38). Not all pedophiles have experienced overt sexual abuse, but most have felt rejected in their attempts to secure love and attention from caregivers, especially maternal figures. In their pedophilic acts, they seem to express their desire to control or get revenge while gratifying their sexual drive.

Men who have been physically as well as sexually abused have some tendency to be both physically abusive and more sexually inconsiderate toward their female partners. Some men who were seduced by dominating females remain more or less impotent, sometimes celibate, apparently as a result of an unconscious fear of being infantalized and engulfed. This fear may also be accompanied by fear of destructive hostility toward women. The aversion toward women can easily develop into latent or overt homosexual tendencies in order to satisfy basic libidinal desires for closeness and sexuality. When men who have had incest with their mothers show signs of severe neurotic disorder, or even of psychosis, the psychopathology seems more related to persistence of unresolved early symbiotic attachment to the mother and lack of separation than simply to the sexual events themselves. The mothers, too, seem to be reluctant to let their sons separate and individuate.

Boys sexually maltreated by males are more reluctant than are girls to talk about their experiences. They are likely to feel great shame over having been manipulated, unassertive, submissive, and being less than truly masculine. Their male identity is very shaky, and they wonder if they are homosexual. The associated feeling that women are not reliably loving and the consequent turning to men for basic love of course contributes to the vulnerability to abuse and to the homosexual problem.

Like men, sexually abused women have various sexual dysfunctions. Dyspareunia and vaginismus are frequent. Some women remain celibate and never have anything to do with men, while others relate well with homosexual men, who are no threat to them. Some, still yearning for maternal love and angry at abusive men, enter into more or less overt lesbian relationships.

Some marry and have superficially normal lives but remain uneasy or frigid in sexual relations. They have trouble raising their children and providing adequate sex education and protection for them. Many mothers of incested girls have themselves been victims of incest and other abuse. Despite their own victimization, they often seem unable to protect their daughters from incest and may even subtly encourage it (Meiselman, 1978). The mother may have repressed her own abuse and denied the possibility of its occurring with her own child. Her diminished ability to be adequately empathic and caring of her child may cause feelings of neglect and yearning for love that lead the daughter to turn to the more available father for care and attention; the mother's inability to enjoy or allow sexual activity may encourage a vulnerable, needy husband to seek out his daughter. The mutual need for emotional closeness can lead to a sexualized relationship, with the daughter submissively obedient to the father's selfish, exploitative behavior. It is a mistake to confuse this situation with an actualization of ordinary oedipal fantasies.

CASE EXAMPLE

The following case is a bit more blatant than average, and although it encompasses a degree of pathology not ordinarily seen in patients who undergo analysis, it is not atypical in the general scene it portrays of some of the problems in the sexual abuse of children.

Henry, a 35-year-old blue-collar worker reported voluntarily to social service and law enforcement that he was concerned about his sexual behaviors and wanted help. He and his wife, Carrie, had a very dependent, clinging marital relationship with periodic disappointments and separations. They had had some involvement with other swingers and occasional wife swapping. For two years they had involved their son, Pete, now 10, in their sexual activities: father and son in mutual oral, genital relationships and mother and son in genital intercourse and oral-genital interactions. Pete had also begun intercourse with the daughter of family friends. All this was done in the name of showing love and closeness. Carrie had been adopted after being physically abused and neglected by her biological parents and was further abused by a foster brother. She had many psychosomatic complaints and was rather pathetic and sickly. Henry had married her partially out of sympathy and wished to care for her.

Henry had been abused and neglected by an alcoholic, Fundamentalist minister father, who himself had been abused by his mother. Henry's mother had been sexually abused by her father, uncles, and brother. She and Henry were quite close. He helped her with housework when she was sickly or while she worked as a nurse in a Veterans' Hospital. They often comforted each other in the attempt to substitute for father's lack of care and attention. They finally had mutually enjoyable sexual intercourse beginning when he was 10 and lasting until he was 12. He described it as a wonderful, beautiful experience with a pleasure he had thought to recapture in later life but had never found. After mother's death from pulmonary disease, father remarried and sent Henry and his sister out of the house to live with grandmother, who physically and verbally abused Henry as she had abused his father. Henry also had sexual relations with a new half-sister and a cousin. While working as a supply officer in the Marines during the Viet Nam War, Henry had some homosexual relationships and also became involved with a rather bereft woman in Manila for whom he bought a house and provided support. He left her when she tried to murder him in order to get his government insurance.

In this skeletal family history, one can easily see the transgenerational transmission of maladaptive patterns of the parent--child relationships that are found in all types of child abuse. Common in families in which maltreatment occurs is that both parents are products of similarly unhappy backgrounds.

We consider the transgenerational repetition of aberrant sexual behaviors to be on one level the normal process of children identifying with parents and simply repeating their patterns of parent-child interactions. As some fathers say very clearly, "My father slept with all of my sisters, so why shouldn't I have sex with my daughters?" On a more unconscious level, in addition to identification with the aggressor, there is an analogous identification with the sexual seducer in an effort to maintain ego integrity through activity rather than passivity. This identification was exemplified by a six-year-old girl who, after being raped, announced, "When I grow up, I am going to be a boy and hurt girls" (Dr. Ruth Kempe, personal communication). There is routinely also an identification with the unempathic caregiver of early life that enables the perpetrator of sexual maltreatment to be oblivious of the victim's needs and state. Being reared by unempathic parents leaves a child unable to be adequately empathic with either self or others. In some dysfunctional families, the child grows up in a chaotic, sexually overstimulating milieu and comes to believe that such behaviors are "normal"—"It's just the way life is."

As noted earlier, sexual trauma often leaves the child confused and unable to fully trust his own perceptions. The unsureness of what is reality and confusion about right and wrong are aggravated by what Ferenczi (1933) spoke of as parental "double talk." An example is the father who in friendly fashion coerced his son into performing fellatio and then beat the boy for doing an unacceptable, dirty sexual act. Kramer (1983) has also described serious confusion in the victim's mind and how the doubts can be used in a defensive manner as well as to instigate ongoing, aggressive, and sexual behaviors. Doubts and confusion can also seriously interfere with the development of identity, as exemplified by an incestuous father who often said to his early teenage daughter, "If you get pregnant, we'll kick you out of the family," and at other times, "Since you never get pregnant, you must be no good as a woman." From earliest childhood he repeatedly called her "ugly" and "fat." Under such circumstances, any valid identity as a female with potential reproductive pleasure is well nigh impossible.

Probably the most tragic sequel to sexual abuse is the pervasive, depressive feeling that one can never enter into a comfortable adult life and that rewarding, intimate relationships are impossible to achieve. Any attempt to be close with another person is perceived as dangerous. Even more distressing is the lack of a coherent sense of self; and the sense that whatever fragments of a self exist are degraded, unacceptable, or worthless. Life is thought of as an endless, bleak, isolated loneliness, which one patient described as "like living in a Kafka novel."

Attempts to develop adult relationships end in trouble, often with additional experience of maltreatment. It is common to see expressions of what we classify as the moral masochism that Berliner (1947) aptly described as attachment to sadistic love objects, for example, in the battered spouse syndrome or other forms of submission to exploitation in jobs or general living. Trying to live sometimes becomes too hopeless and painful, and suicidal behaviors occur. Another impetus toward suicide is the victim's unconscious identification with the abusers of early years and the repetition of their behavior. One is just as bad as the hated parent whom one wanted to kill, so one needs to kill oneself.

Shengold (1979) described the damage to the psyche of abused children as "soul murder," and it is true that maltreatment victims often feel as if the very core of their being has been destroyed. Soul murder seems to be more severe in girl incest victims, for the sexual penetration is perceived as a destructive invasion of the innermost body, the ultimate invasion of privacy, much worse than verbal abuse or physical attacks on the body surface. As one young woman described it, "I always thought I could grow up and get away from all the beatings and criticism and then be free to live. But when my father overpowered me and put his penis in my vagina, it was the end. All hope was gone. My spirit had been killed. And mother did not care. That's when I cut my wrists."

In recent years the increasing awareness of and concern over the sexual abuse of children has sparked investigations of its occurrence in the general population of psychiatric patients. Husain and Chapel (1983) found that of 437 adolescent girls admitted to a psychiatric hospital for emotional problems, 61 reported an incestuous involvement. In a study of 188 psychiatric inpatients, Carman, Rieder, and Mills (1984) found that 15 had been sexually abused and another 23 had been both physically and sexually assaulted. Bryer et al. (1987) reported that 44% of a sample of 66 female psychiatric inpatients described sexual abuse before age 16. Jacobson and Richardson (1987) found on detailed inquiry into the histories of 100 psychiatric inpatients that 81 had experienced major physical or sexual assaults. They also noted previous therapists' lack of awareness of these assaults and recommended routine inquiry into patients' assault history. A study of 60 women with somatization disorder revealed that 55% of them had been sexually molested (Morrison, 1989). The diagnostic criteria for posttraumatic stress disorder were met by 20% of the sexually abused children investigated by Deblinger and colleagues (1989). Seventeen women patients who had experienced childhood or adolescent incest presented symptoms that fit the features of posttraumatic stress disorder (Lindberg and Distad, 1985).

Patients who are diagnosed as having borderline and narcissistic personality disorders frequently give histories of deprivation, physical abuse, and sexual abuse, although such events are not always recognized as significant etiological factors. Persons with multiple personality disorder commonly have histories of maltreatment, especially sexual abuse (Kluft, 1985). More often, less drastic denial and "partial" dissociation are seen as defense mechanisms in abuse victims. Strikingly reminiscent of Freud's early work on hysteria nearly a century ago are recent reports of hysterical seizures as sequels of incest (Goodwin, Simms, and Bergman, 1979; Gross, 1979).

It must not be assumed from these reports of an association between psychiatric disorders and previous sexual abuse that this is a simple, direct, cause-and-effect relationship. The sexual events do not occur as isolated events in an otherwise "good enough" environment; they are typically the more dramatic and traumatic episodes in an otherwise chaotic, depriving milieu of inadequate, distorted caregiving. The sexual exploitation, however, can become the focal point, the experience around which all other deleterious happenings are clustered and organized in the victim's psychic functioning.

As Anna Freud (1965) said, "Due to their inability to care for themselves, infants and children have to put up with whatever care is given them" (p. 155). Children living in psychologically chaotic families are inevitably traumatized by the combination of excessive, unmanageable stimulation and the lack of protection and ego support from their caregivers. Not only are psychosexual development and later sexual behaviors markedly distorted, but the development of a basic sense of self and of a valid identity, good reality testing, and nonconflicted superego functions are seriously impaired.

REFERENCES

Berliner, B. (1947), On some psychodynamics of masochism. *Psychoanal. Quart.* 16:459–471.

Bryer, J. B., Nelson, B. A., Miler, J. B. & Krol, P. (1987), Childhood sexual and physical abuse as factors in adult psychiatric illness. *Amer. J. Psychiat.*, 144:1426–1430.

Cantwell, H. (1988), Child abuse: Very young perpetrators. *Child Abuse & Neglect*, 12:579–582.

Carmen, E., Rieder, P., & Mills, T. (1984), Victims of violence and psychiatric illness. *Amer. J. Psychiat.*, 141:378–383.

Deblinger, E., McLeer, S., Atkins, M., Ralphe, D. & Foa, E. (1989), Post-traumatic stress in sexually abused, physically abused, and nonabused children. *Child Abuse & Neglect*, 13:403–408.

De Salvo, L. (1989), *Virginia Woolf: The Impact of Childhood Sexual Abuse on Her Life and Work.* Boston: Beacon Press.

Ferenczi, S. (1933), The confusion of tongues between the adult and the child. *Internat. J. Psycho-Anal.*, 30:225–230.

Freud, A. (1965), *Normality and Pathology in Childhood.* New York: International Universities Press.

Goodwin, J., Simms, M. & Bergman, R. (1979), Hysterical seizures: A sequel to incest. *Amer. J. Orthopsychiat.*, 49:698–703.

Gross, M. (1979), Incestuous rape: A cause for hysterical seizures in four adolescent girls. *Amer. J. Orthopsychiat.*, 49:704–708.

Husain, A. & Chapel, J. (1983), History of incest in girls admitted to a psychiatric hospital. *Amer. J. Psychiat.*, 140:591–593.

Johnson, T. (1989), Female child perpetrators: Children who molest other children. *Child Abuse & Neglect*, 13:571–585.

Jacobson, A. & Richardson, B. (1987), Assault experiences of 100 psychiatric impatients: Evidence of the need for routine inquiry. *Amer. J. Psychiat*, 144:908–913.

Kluft, R., ed. (1985), *Childhood Antecedents of Multiple Personality.* Washington, DC: American Psychiatric Press.

Kramer, S. (1983), Object-coercive doubting: A pathological defensive response to maternal incest. *J. Amer. Psychoanal. Assn.*, Supl. 31:325–351.

Lindberg, F. & Distad, L. (1985), Post-traumatic stress disorders in women who experienced childhood incest. *Child Abuse & Neglect*, 9:329–334.

Litin, E., Griffin, M. & Johnson, A. (1956), Parental influence in unusual sexual behavior in children. *Psychoanal Quart.*, 25:37–55.

Meiselman, K. C. (1978), *Incest*. San Francisco: Jossey Bass.

Morrison, J. (1989), Childhood sexual histories of women with somatization disorder. *Amer. J. Psychiat.*, 146:239–241.

Shengold, L. (1979), Child abuse and deprivation: Soul murder. *J. Amer. Psychoanal. Assn.*, 27:533–557.

Steele, B. F. & Alexander, H. (1981), Long term effects of sexual abuse in childhood. In: *Sexually Abused Children and Their Families*, ed. P. B. Mrazek & C. H. Kempe. New York: Pergamon, pp. 233–234.

Waelder, R. (1960), *Basic Theory of Psychoanalysis*. New York: International Universities Press.

3

The Psychoanalysis of Adults Who Were Sexually Abused In Childhood:
A Preliminary Report from the Discussion Group of the American Psychoanalytic Association

J. Alexis Burland
Raymond Raskin

Since 1985, a series of discussion groups has been held in conjunction with the mid-winter meetings of the American Psychoanalytic Association on the topic of the psychoanalysis of adults who experienced sexual abuse in childhood. Some 30 to 40 psychoanalysts have attended each meeting at which clinical material ranging from brief clinical vignettes to formal presentations of completed or nearly completed analyses have been presented. This chapter summarizes what has come out of those meetings. Much work needs to be done; consequently, what has been concluded to date must be viewed as preliminary and therefore tentative.

Several questions have been posed in an effort to offer direction to the discussions. As sexual abuse is always "but one tree in the forest," how can one conceptualize and understand its specific contribution to neurosogenesis? What is the role of the age, or, more precisely, the developmental level, of the child? Are there clinical symptoms pathognomonic of childhood sexual abuse? How does a history of sexual abuse correlate with analyzability? Are there specific problems unique to the analyses of adults who have suffered sexual abuse?

Although some kind of sexual/genital fondling or play is almost universal in childhood, most such experiences are not psychologically traumatic. What makes an experience traumatic and therefore an instance of true "abuse" is a complex issue. Whether or not an experience is traumatic depends primarily on the capacity of the child's as yet immature ego to cope with the experience. This capacity reflects both the child's own psychological developmental accomplishments to date and the nature of the child's relationships with the primary objects who function as auxiliary egos as needed. Since any overwhelming actual experience can stimulate or conform to already anxiety-provoking drive-derived fantasies, the sexually abused child's ego can be pressured from within as well as from without, upsetting both id-ego and ego-reality balances. Consequences may not only be immediate but may have the potential for continuing impact on the course of the child's development, with the possibility of permanently skewed psychic structuralization. In general, the earlier the abuse, the greater its potential impact because of the immaturity and plasticity of the ego. Our case material suggests that if abuse occurs prior to the completion of separation-individuation—say, before the age of three—self–other boundaries can remain undifferentiated and severe character pathology, including the possibility of a sexual perversion, can result.

When the abuser is a primary object—a parent or other close relative—the impact is greater not only because of the intensity of the relationship, but because the abuser is also one of the persons to whom the child turns for support. Owing to the child's anaclitic attachment to the parents, each instance of abuse is an indication of a failure of that parent in his or her role as protector for the child. This failure has its own pathogenic impact and may be played out in all aspects of day-to-day living. Indeed, it is very often the emotionally abandoned child, desperate for libidinal supplies, who is most easily victimized by an abuser.

At the same time, clinical experience also suggests a particular vulnerability for the phallic-oedipal child. That child is—or often imagines himself or herself to be—an active participant in the abuse and is therefore likely to carry away from the experience a burden of guilt and responsibility. Such a child may have a neurotic structure to the remnants of the experience, with neurotic guilt and clinical indications of unconscious conflict.

For children who were abused at an earlier age, at a time when dependent attachments with their ego developmental consequences were more central, the eventual clinical picture would more likely reflect deviant ego development and problems with object relationships.

Where the parents are less than "good enough" (Winnicott, 1960, p. 145) the fusion of the good parent and the bad parent imagos can be impeded, with the resultant persistence of some degree of splitting. The greater the admixture of aggression or violence in the abusive act, the greater the challenge to the ego. The result is likely to be a failure in the ego's capacity for neutralization. The more frequent the abuse, the greater the drain on the child's resources, not to mention the greater the failure of the parents to serve as protectors for the child. Even more significant is how the family responds to the abusive situations; if, as happens all too often, they deny that anything happened—or even accuse the child of lying—the child's capacity for reality testing can become impaired.

Ironically, if the abuse is discovered, the resultant family strife, physical exams (often intrusive in nature because of the anatomy involved), psychiatric evaluations—often including the use of overstimulating "anatomically correct" (i.e., genital) dolls—and court hearings can be as traumatic as the original sexual abuse itself. These same factors can also be traumatic for the child's support systems, that is, the immediate family, who can end up being less available and less supportive when needed the most.

There is almost always an enormous tendency for fantasy elaborations of the experience, both at the time the abuse occured and later, especially around the time of entry into a new developmental phase, with its new perspectives and revisions of memories of the past. Thus, fact and fantasy can be very difficult to differentiate. This confusion is what Freud wrote of (1896, p. 168–; 1897, pp. 259–260). He never abandoned the idea that actual sexual abuse could, and often did, happen to children and that such experiences could be the basis for later symptom neuroses; he had, however, to confront the clinical fact that it was not always possible to say with certainty what was fact and what was fantasy in any individual instance.

A wide spectrum of presenting symptoms and degrees of psychopathology can accompany a history of sexual abuse. Diagnoses may range from psychotic through "normal neurotic," and the patients may be analyzable, difficult to analyze, or unanalyzable. There are too many variables to allow for generalizations about treatability. These patients do, however, reveal certain features once treatment is under way. The features may not be pathognomonic, but their presence should alert the therapist to consider the possibility that sexual abuse has occurred. Castration fears seem unusually intense. Often there are repetitive and traumatic dreams. These patients need to distance themselves from others. There is a basic depressive affect. There are also periods of cognitive confusion and dissociative states, particularly when, during the course of the analytic process, previously repressed memories of the abusive experiences are being recovered. Patients doubt their own associations, feel unable to differentiate between fantasies and actual memories of real events, and complain of a need to disbelieve their own thoughts. Freud's (1896, 1897) comments that it is difficult to tell whether or not actual abuse occurred may have stemmed from this phenomenon in the patients he was treating. Among the cases presented in the discussion groups, some patients, who had a long history of more than adequate reality testing and function in life, had gone through a period when they seemed almost borderline in their functioning as their grasp on reality collapsed and their self-doubting and confusion intensified; some even experienced what seemed to be transference psychoses. Once their memories were recovered and acknowledged, the patients' mental status rapidly reverted to its previous, more adequate condition.

As already indicated, when the sexual abuser is a parent, the developmental impact is usually greater than when the abuser is someone else. Because they need to protect the dependent tie to the "good enough" side of the parent while simultaneously protecting themselves from the abusing side of the same parent, many of these patients develop a defensive splitting that spills over into all their relationships. If this split involves the self-image as well, the groundwork may then be laid for the development of a multiple personality disorder, a condition often associated with a history of abuse. Some victims of abuse identify with the abusive parent and as adults become abusers themselves or fear that they will. Overstimulation at the hands of a primary object can lead to incomplete self–object differentiation and to failure in the development of an observing ego. Problems often surround the sense of ownership of one's body, related to its being used for the pleasures of the parent.

All these factors affect the relationship with the analyst or therapist. The sense of abandonment by the protector-parent interferes with the development of trust and therefore can interfere with the working alliance. Patients often fear that the therapist will sexually abuse them or will perceive their recalling and reliving of the sexually abusive experiences, or elements of the necessary transference regression, as a real sexual seduction. The projection onto the therapist of the neglectful or abusing parent introject can lead to the preponderance of a negative transference. In other cases, an erotized masochistic transference may act as a stubborn resistance. Because of these difficulties in establishing and maintaining an adequate positive transference, some patients may benefit from, or require, an initial period of vis-à-vis psychotherapy.

An important dimension in predicting the outcome of treatment is the degree to which the memories of the past sexual abuse are revived in an effort at belated mastery, as opposed to the extent to which they are revived to be actualized as part of an id resistance. Both forms of repetition usually coexist although their ratio varies.

Countertransference problems regularly arise. For instance, the therapist may feel guilt or anxiety at being placed in the seductive role of helping the patient recall and relive memories of the sexually abusive and traumatic experiences. And, too, there is a tendency for the therapist to become overinvolved in the details of the often "hair raising" traumatic experiences. As a result, there is the risk of overlooking the dynamically more important intrapsychic aspects of the experiences. Some patients play into this tendency, which may exist in others as well as therapists, by seeking and finding narcissistic gratification in the shock reactions they evoke when they describe what happened to them. Consequently, their reports become elaborated and ornamented over time, so that fact and fantasy are further obscured. In addition—and perhaps related to patients' own doubts about their memories—therapists may note a reluctance in themselves to hear evidence in the patients' productions that such abuse actually occurred.

Several generalizations emerged from the extensive clinical reports presented and discussed at the meetings. In most of the cases, memories of the experiences of abuse had been repressed prior to treatment and were recaptured only during the course of analysis. In those instances where patients did recall the sexual abuse prior to treatment and included it in their initial history, aspects of the trauma, especially the more powerful affects associated with the abuse, had been repressed. Unfortunately, at this point our data do not yet permit us to understand or even hypothesize why some patients fail to repress memories of their childhood sexual trauma while others are able to do so.

Although the range of historical events and family patterns presented varied, there was a pattern that we discerned and that might be considered prototypical. A depressed, and therefore libidinally unavailable, mother left both father and daughter feeling deprived. In addition, the daughter evolved an altruistic mode of interaction in dealing with the mother's depression, seeing her role as that of mother's caretaker or "therapist." Thus, the daughter's hunger for love, and her eagerness to gratify others' needs in order to obtain it, met with father's unsatisfied sexual hungers. In each case studied, the family pattern was marked by repression, with subsequent acting out of that which had been repressed. This pattern was reinforced and accompanied by the habitual use of lies, secrets, denials, and instructions to the children not to tell this or that person this or that piece of information. Complaints were often responded to with, "It's just your imagination." This pattern pervaded not only the incidents of sexual abuse, but many dimensions of the family's interactions. In those few cases where the abuser was not a parent—for example, a teen-age cousin who acted as the child's baby sitter—these features were still in evidence, though often to a lesser degree.

In terms of technique, our cases suggest that the underlying maternal deprivation—including the remnants of the less than adequate protection against overstimulation—needed to be analyzed first; then memories of the abusive experiences would surface. The most likely explanation for this sequence is that the successful analysis and working through of the negative dyadic transference strengthens the working alliance and the positive transference, thereby offering support to the patient's ego and making it possible for the patient to confront the intense and painfully disruptive affects associated with the memories of sexual abuse.

As a final note, we would like to emphasize that in spite of the complexity of these cases and the many difficulties encountered, most participants in the discussion groups reported cases that had responded well to psychoanalysis. With all due respect for the problems of self-selection, we feel, on the basis of our experience, that analysis is indicated and potentially of enormous benefit in the treatment of adults who were sexually abused as children.

REFERENCES

Freud, S. (1896), Further remarks on the neuro-psychoses of defence. *Standard Edition*, 3: 159–188. London: Hogarth Press, 1962.

_____ (1897), Extracts from the Fliess papers. *Standard Edition*, 1: 175–283. London: Hogarth Press, 1966.

Winnicott, D. W. (1960), Ego distortions in terms of true and false self. In: *The Maturational Process and the Facilitating Environment*. New York: International Universities Press, pp. 140–152, 1965.

Clinical Considerations and Psychoanalytic Process

4

Technical Issues of the Opening Phase

David L. Raphling

The initial phase of psychoanalysis with an adult patient whose background includes a childhood or adolescent history of incest assumes, as in all analyses, a distinctive pattern derived from the unique combination of analyst and patient at work. The psychoanalytic situation, though utilizing a standard and fundamental method and procedure, is ultimately influenced by the patient's personality and psychopathology, as well as by the analyst's own psychology and his theoretical and technical biases. The product of these factors in any given analytic dyad will determine how and when the analytic process will be initiated. The effect of incest trauma on personality and psychopathology can range from minor disturbances in function to severe psychic disorganization. Some incest victims with perilously weakened mental structure bring to the opening phase much less potential for engaging the analytic situation than do others whose psychic structure and function may have been less disturbed.

Sexually abused patients often enter analysis with more trepidation than do other patients because their traumatic life experiences have alerted them to danger and sensitized them in the sphere of intimate relationships. The regression necessary for free association within the analytic situation requires suspension of censorship and relaxation of certain ego controls and defensive postures. This relaxation can be accomplished by the patient only in an atmosphere of trust, where uncertainty and ambiguity can be experienced and tolerated with a prevailing sense of security. The strain on their ability to partially abrogate their habitual protective stance and defensive strategies for the purpose of psychoanalytic inquiry is particularly great for patients whose bodily integrity, autonomy, and sense of self have been violated in incestuous relationships.

Patients with a background of incest enter analysis for a variety of reasons. At one extreme, certain patients begin analysis without any memory of past incestuous experience, whereas others' sole conscious impetus for analysis stems from having endured sexual abuse. Patients for whom the incest barrier has been transgressed view the often desperately needed treatment as a possibly devastating repetition of the trauma; they believe that in any situation incestuous fantasy may again become reality. The motivation for treatment may be impaired in those for whom childhood incestuous experience was registered and elaborated as a traumatic psychic reality. These patients are reluctant to engage in a procedure that threatens to revive events whose intrapsychic meaning may have had a powerful, and often profoundly damaging, effect on their psychic integrity. Resistance is especially noticeable when features inherent in the analytic situation or those created through fantasy enactment by the patient seem to mirror closely any aspect of the original traumatic experience. For these patients, the decision to embark on analytic treatment carries with it a certain sense of danger that looms as the background of the opening phase and beyond.

CASE EXAMPLES

AV, a 40-year-old single woman, sought analysis for severe depression and began work with a female analyst. She had been severely traumatized during her prepubertal years when her father touched her breasts and repeatedly urged her to fondle and suck his penis. The patient began analysis feeling helpless and anxious. She actively sought protection and support from the analyst, whom she idealized as a nurturing figure. The patient's dependence on this idealized image of the analyst reflected her wish and need for an unambivalent relationship with an available maternal figure unlike her own alcoholic, depressed mother. Her mother was an unreliable caretaking figure, who may have encouraged her husband's incestuous activity with the patient. AV had looked in vain to her mother for protection from her father's seductive and abusive behavior. She encountered, instead, unpredictable maternal behavior: emotional unavailability and an irrationally critical attitude. It soon became clear, however, that the most crucial aspect of her need for the analyst to protect her from images of her abusive parents was a deep mistrust of her own part in the incestuous behavior. She indicated this mistrust by looking to her analyst for approval of her choices of men to date and permission to become sexually involved with them.

Hatred of both parents and an enormous fear of punishment as a consequence of incestuous involvement appeared as frightening to her as her forbidden sexual wishes. The danger of her destructive impulses prompted her defensively to idealize the analyst and to use splitting to maintain an "all good" image of the analyst early in the analysis.

It was not long before the analyst became the focus of the patient's erotic sensitivity as subtle but unambiguously sexualized derivatives of the idealizing transference emerged in the form of an intense curiosity about the analyst and intrusive attempts to befriend her outside the confines of the analytic setting. Defensive regression to preoedipal wishes emphasizing nurture and support then became more evident as these incestuous strivings produced anxiety and depressive affect.

The patient's seductiveness was apparent in the opening phase as she attempted to go beyond the limits described by the analytic situation. She was able to stimulate the analyst's interest in the graphic details of her incestuous experiences enough so that the analyst's aroused curiosity triumphed over evenly hovering listening, and temporary lapses of neutrality occurred. She found the analyst's probing sexually stimulating, and she was excited by the analyst's occasionally sharp reactions to teasing and intrusiveness. Her wish for sexual gratification from the analyst, however, conflicted with her need to make certain that she was safe with an analyst who, unlike her parents, could resist her seductive pressures.

Another woman, BD began analysis with me soon after a long and largely satisfactory period of analysis with a female analyst ended when the patient moved from another city to take advantage of a professional opportunity. BD had been fondled and masturbated by her mother until age 14 "for as long as I could remember." She had been in casts for her first year and a half or two years for a minor congenital deformity of her lower extremities. The caretaking requirements of this situation became an early focus of her mother's preoccupation with her body, a focus that later became frankly sexual. The mother's intrusive concern with the patient's bowel habits and general hygiene showed itself through enemas and manual manipulation of anal and genital orifices in the name of cleanliness. This manipulation, and the later masturbation, caused BD to feel as if her mother "possessed" her body, which she could not "own" herself. She felt that her mother had invaded her mind as well as her body. Mother's sexual interest in her, however, alternated with utter rejection, which often caused her to feel that she did not even exist apart from being an object of her mother's sexual exploitation. Although she had been passive in relation to the repeated sexual stimulation, and enraged and deeply resentful of her mother for it, she had discovered in her previous analysis that she had also sought out and enjoyed the incestuous sexual contact.

Having difficulty working out the logistics of scheduling and fees, BD began her analysis with a great deal of resistance. She very much wanted to begin the analysis, but this venture stirred up her anxiety and, with it, reactivated her dependency on her first analyst, whom she again consulted. At first she could attribute her anxiety only to being "uncomfortable" with me "for some reason." Each session made her stomach rumble audibly, which embarrassed her and had never occurred in the previous analysis. She was not sure she could trust me even though I did not actually appear to give her cause for concern.

From the first, BD acted almost inappropriately friendly and always greeted me with an innocent but enigmatic smile that seemed simultaneously to express and to belie her apprehension. She realized that she had been thrown off balance by me because, unlike her first analyst, I was a relatively young-appearing man toward whom she could be physically attracted. Though this realization threatened her, she was also conscious of how attractive she might be to me and appeared freshly made up and perfumed for her sessions. Her smile began to lose its innocence and became seductive. On entering and taking leave, she stared at me intently and several times asked why I had such a "strange" look. Inquiry revealed that strange meant sexual, which was exactly what her own staring and smile had seemed to me. I raised the possibility that she was unwittingly reading into her perception of me something of her own expression. She acknowledged having had a sexual interest in me from our initial meeting and was quite possibly looking at me in a seductive way, but she could not shake the idea that there was "something" about the way I looked at her. As a consequence of this interchange I became more conscious of how I looked at her and realized that I had been drawn into looking at her more closely than is usual for me. She feared she had been sexually provocative without realizing it when I acknowledged that indeed I must have been staring at her. She said that she had been having conscious sexual fantasies about me, something she had never encountered with her female analyst. BD had felt safe from sexual interest in her first analyst, though she did not know why, considering that her incestuous involvement had been with a woman.

She briefly developed a stiff neck, which she attributed to restraining herself from looking at me, though this symptom had other, deeper meanings related to her feeling of having been used as a phallus for her mother's pleasure. She later connected the stiff neck with memories of her legs in braces when her mother began to molest her. She had a fantasy of me undressing her, medically examining her neck, and touching her in ways that would be sexually arousing. BD believed she must explore these fantasies and feelings to complete the analytic work begun with her first analyst. I realized that she also imagined this sexual material would intrigue me. But she feared the associative process would lead to a loss of control and said, "Whenever I let my sexual feelings be known to mom, she took me up on them." I interpreted to her that the conscious memory of her mother's seduction was less threatening at the moment than what she now wished to avoid—the possibility of seducing me.

From the beginning of the analysis, BD frequently interrupted me when I intervened with interpretations. It now became clear that my interventions, like her mother's sexual advances, seemed exciting, but "scary," because they were not under her control. She was not aware of feeling angry even when she experienced my interventions as intrusions that diminished her seductive power over me.

As the analysis progressed we learned that BD's almost immediate, somewhat exaggerated sexual interest was also a reaction against having hostile impulses toward me that were instead displaced to her current boyfriend.

Projective mechanisms and ambiguity concerning the internal versus external origin of transference wishes and superego criticism in the opening phase were even more pronounced in another patient, CW, whose difficulty differentiating aspects of self from object directly reflected her suspicion of having been sexually abused by her father during childhood. Though she was convinced of this, she had no conscious memory of any incestuous experiences. The patient did not mention the possibility of paternal incest until treatment was well underway. She was ashamed of having such an idea, especially if it were untrue. She would then really have to view herself as "perverse." On the surface she minimized the notion that incest could have actually occurred, and she began exploring unconscious conflicts activated by her recent marriage. She had initially sought psychotherapy some months prior to her wedding because of trepidation about marriage. After a brief period of dynamic psychotherapy, we agreed that psychoanalysis would be the best treatment for her. She had been in therapy with a female analyst since late adolescence, when she was in turmoil, became pregnant, and was experimenting with drugs. She stated that she had successfully avoided discussing sexual matters with her analyst and, as far as she could remember, did not mention the possibility of having had incestuous experiences.

This topic came up when in the course of our work CW began to feel "intimidated" by me to a degree that she realized was exaggerated: she had a persistent feeling that I would find her attractive and want to take advantage of her. She felt that I, and other men in her life in positions of authority, had sexual designs on her; and though she realized this could not possibly be true, she still felt anxious around me and other men. She was aware of feeling attracted to me and acknowledged fantasies of allowing me to seduce her. Meanwhile she struggled with ambivalent feelings toward her husband, who she feared was "a wimp" and perhaps homosexual, definitely neurotic, and self-centered. CW felt that her husband's treatment of her was erratic: he could be close and warm with her one minute and cold, critical, and rejecting the next. In sexual relations, she often felt he was using her for his own gratification without regard to her feelings.

CW would come for most of the hours in a state of agitation and tears. She was feeling like a helpless victim, at the mercy of her husband, others at work, and her family, who she believed were directly critical of her or made disparaging remarks about and references to her. She wanted to look within herself for the source of her marital problems (if for no other reason than to please me), but she was convinced that her husband was largely to blame. She complained that I, like everyone else, doubted that her father had abused her. I interpreted that now she could feel similarly abused and denied by me if she thought I did not believe her. While privately considering how her insistence on a traumatic event could prove to be a resistance to analyzing intrapsychic motives, I maintained an inquiring attitude, be-lieving everything and believing nothing regarding the possi-bility that paternal incest had actually occurred.

CW's father had been a victim of incest himself. He had been sexually molested by his paternal grandfather at the age of 12 and was then sent away by the family to boarding school. He was severely depressed and a chronic alcoholic during CW's child-hood. He had been devastated by the birth of a congenitally deformed son born six years after CW and had divorced her mother two years later. The father died of alcoholic cirrhosis when CW graduated college.

As she spoke of her father on several occasions during hours, CW's eyes began to tear, but in the absence of emotion. This occurred once when she was recalling a dream of the previous night "of a man who gets into the house and is under the bed. He has broken in, but also he had the keys and that was how he got in. He was scuzzy—but then he seemed very nice. When he leaves I get new locks for the doors." This dream reminded her of another dream, of a man breaking into their house through the window. The house in the dream was her father's, where she visited him after his divorce from her mother when the patient was eight. "The man seemed cuckoo brained. What an odd, juvenile expression, but that's what came to mind." "Cuckoo brained" meant that "he acted unpredictably: nice one minute and disgusting the next. It makes me sick to my stomach: like throwing up. Somehow we were at a table eating. I don't understand. Mother was in the background." She said her father was unpredictable, out of control when drunk, usually passing out. She recalled having driven across an icy bridge in winter fearing that she would lose control and surprising herself by crying aloud, "I won't tell." She now wondered if this referred to something illicit with her father. She felt that her husband used her for sex. Sex smothered her. She felt repulsed and disgusted as she did in the dream. In the next hour she had an image of a threatening man standing behind her with an erect penis. This led to feelings of being trapped, of grossness, and a flash thought of performing oral sex on me. This and other material certainly made consideration of actual paternal incest plausible, though she has not yet uncovered any memory of incest.

DISCUSSION

The opening phase of analysis is literally an introduction. It is a joining of two strangers in a shared experience of growing intimacy in which they are bound at the end to become more intimate strangers. From the beginning, they want to know everything about one another. Though the patient looks to psychoanalysis as a way to achieve profound self-knowledge, she also strives to know more of her analyst. This need to make out the analyst behind his screen of anonymity, a powerful motive for all patients, is absolutely compelling for a patient whose parents directly or indirectly violated an intimate relationship by permitting incestuous fantasies to become realities.

For abused patients there is a blurring of distinctions between important aspects of self and other (Kramer, 1983), between instinctual wishes and seductive external pressures, and between guilt and innocence (Shengold, 1980). Patients bring to their analyses the atmosphere of ambiguity, denial, and distortion in which incest was consummated. They confront these dangers in the opening phase with anxiety, mistrust, hypervigilence, and even hostility toward the analyst, though they hope for the protection and support of a benign analyst whose image will contrast with those of both the abusing parent and the parent who failed to shield them from abuse (Steele, 1986). In the introductory phase, patients need to assure themselves of the analyst's respect for their psychic and bodily integrity. As in all analyses, the basic conditions for this assurance and protection are the analyst's nonintrusive empathic inquiry and his cogent, well-timed, appropriate interpretations. On occasion, however, these conditions alone are not sufficient for patients otherwise deemed suitable for analysis to overcome their apprehension concerning the dangers aroused by beginning analysis. They may require some modification of the analyst's technique in order to establish an analytic process.

Patient BD's previous analyst had established her analytic sessions on a thrice-weekly schedule, which the patient has been unwilling to change in her analysis with me. This resistance reflects the many conflicts stimulated by having to exchange her previous analyst for me. Now, after almost two years of her analysis with me, she remains ambivalently reluctant to increase the frequency of her sessions. This restriction has extended beyond the opening phase, and along with her habitual tardiness to sessions, has been assimilated into her established pattern of transference resistance. The technical modification in the number of sessions has not seemed to preclude the development of an analytic process. Its specific meaning for the patient as a nidus for resistance, as well as its significance for the analyst's transferences, will determine its analyzability and the ultimate fate of the analysis.

The same may be said of patient CW's analysis, which evolved within six months from a trial period of psychoanalytically oriented psychotherapy with limited goals into a standard psychoanalysis. This transition occurred as a result of mutual recognition of the need and suitability for psychoanalysis and our willingness to begin the work. The development of an alliance based on positive transference during the psychotherapy contributed to her request for psychoanalysis, to which I responded affirmatively. While objective considerations of both analyst and patient played a significant role in the decision to begin analysis, the important contribution of transference manifestations, as well as countertransference responses, cannot be underestimated. The apparently benign positive transference, without which the psychoanalysis might not have begun, will continue to affect the course of the analysis beyond the opening phase and may prove to be as much of a resistance as that of patient BD. Stein (1981) has called attention to the ways in which the "unobjectionable part of the transference" can be a formidable resistance. Although a necessary technical modification may lead to unanalyzable resistances, the analyst's commitment to consistent exploration of it with the patient and interpretation of its meaning make it a risk worth taking to assure the progress of the opening phase.

These concrete alterations of prescribed technique are exceptional, though patients' introduction to the one-sided exposure to the relatively anonymous authority that is part of the opening phase prompts their wish to reverse the situation and expose the analyst. They will sound out the analyst's weaknesses and attempt to induce in him a sense of vulnerability analogous to what they themselves have experienced. They attempt to carry the analysis to the analyst and, with the determination of unconscious motives, will challenge what is most accessible: the structure of the psychoanalytic method and situation itself. This inevitable pressure for alteration of the analytic procedure usually arises as a regressive defensive stance against anxiety and narcissistic vulnerability and is seldom the result of a fixed resistance that cannot be managed by the analyst's attunement to the patient's underlying self-protective need.

The momentous encounter of patient and analyst in the

opening phase inevitably disturbs the equilibrium of the in-trapsychic compromise formations of each individual and sets into motion a process of mutual adaptation in which intrapsy-chic compromises are realigned to accommodate the structure of the analysis. Though this is obviously true for the patient, the analyst himself cannot help but adapt his customary use of a standard technique to the unique needs of each patient with whom he begins analysis. From the very beginning, he will be exquisitely sensitive to the state of his interaction with the patient through his most subtle reactions to the patient's person-ality and style, symptoms and past traumatic experiences, and inchoate transferences. Jacobs (Panel, 1989) demonstrated with clinical examples how the flexibility of the analyst's response to these factors in the patient as they are activated in the opening phase is essential to the progress of the analysis. This respon-siveness to the patient is at the heart of analytic exploration and understanding and is often conveyed to the patient through nonverbal communications of tone, manner, gesture, silence, and timing as well as by the verbal content of interpretations. Much of the development of the opening phase is based on the often silent mutual processing of the patient's characterologic and transferential engagement of the analyst's personality and transferences inherent in his analyzing functions. Ultimately, this interactive process must lead to the articulation of useful transference interpretations to assure the patient's security within the analytic situation.

Patients bring to analysis a susceptibility to recreation of past trauma in the intimate analytic relationship. They are extraordi-narily sensitive to the analyst's motives, probe the analyst's responses to them, and are alert to any sign of betrayal. It is essential that the analyst recognize and interpret the aspects of patients' productions that reflect veridical perceptions of the analyst's person or behavior. This insight is especially difficult for an analyst when patients' accurate perceptions of him have been activated by a departure from an analytic position. The image is then much less a pure transference distortion. If the analyst does not keep abreast of how his actual behavior, colored by transference, is affecting the abused patient, acting out may ensue and the working relationship will deteriorate. Such self-awareness is crucial when the analyst's behavior happens to reproduce closely an aspect of the abusing parent's behavior, since the traumatic legacy of childhood incestuous experience is uncertainty and confusion about fantasy and reality (Blum, 1973). These considerations prompted my acknowledgment to patient BD of the correctness of her perception regarding my countertransference response, though my primary focus was on her reactions to my technical lapse and her part in the enactment sequence.

Reality testing, boundary formation, and other ego capacities and superego function are often seriously impaired in the victims of sexual abuse and reflect defects in the ability to distinguish past from present and fantasy from reality. The patients are beset by images of themselves and their incestuous parents as both good and bad; by not knowing about their incestuous experiences and knowing too well about them, and by being simultaneously innocent and guilty. These confusing splits and contradictions are readily carried over into the analytic relationship. Loss of the "as if" quality of transference, and with it the patient's objective capacity for observing intrapsychic function, severely tests the working alliance. The analysis may founder in the opening phase, and an analytic process may never be established unless the patient's maximal capacity for reality testing and objective observation of the transference are reinforced by consistently neutral inquiry and interpretation. Brenner's (1979) comments on the patient's ability to cooperate constructively in analysis are pertinent to the treatment of the sexually abused:

> Whether at the beginning, in the midst, or in the final stages of analysis, timely, accurate interpretations that are based on correct understanding are far more useful in promoting a patient's ability to do his part than is any behavior, however well intentioned, humane, and intuitively compassionate. . . . In analysis, it is best for the patient if one approaches everything analytically [p. 150].

We must realize, however, that the intrapsychic structure of certain sexually abused patients will be so modified as to render them unable to make use of the analytic method as treatment.

The pervasive threat that forbidden fantasy will "degenerate" into reality in the intimate and regressed atmosphere permitted by the analytic situation is especially prominent in those patients for whom the gender of the analyst corresponds to the gender of the incestuous figure of childhood. Katan (1973) reports on a female patient who was sexually abused by a strange man at age five and was, as well, repeatedly seduced by her father into sexual games as a child. Several attempts at analysis with male analysts failed, having been ended abruptly by extremely aggressive and provocative behavior prompted by the patient's unendurable anxiety. She was unable to tolerate being alone with a man, especially if he was behind her, because she had been approached by the stranger from the rear. Her conviction that her anxiety would be more tolerable if she were analyzed by a woman was borne out by her subsequent analytic experience. Another patient, who had engaged in sexual relations with her father over many years, requested her male analyst to refer her to someone of her own sex after only a brief period of treatment (Rascovsky and Rascovsky, 1950).

The influence of the analyst's gender on the emerging analytic process is especially relevant for patients who have had a sexual relationship with a parent. Although analysis can proceed with a patient whose analyst and abusing parent are of the same gender, the distinction between perceptions of the analyst as a realistic object and as the parental image who has violated the incest barrier is easily blurred when transference is intense. The danger of a revival of the incestuous experience becomes more acute in the patient's mind, and this is as true of the hostile transference as of the erotic component. By contrast, resistance to the emergence and recognition of certain transference manifestations can occur when the gender images of the analyst and abusing parent are different. This resistance is crucial since the transference manifestations that reveal the details of the incestuous experience may be ignored or misunderstood when the genders of analyst and abusing parent are not the same. The gender of the transference image imposed on the analyst is usually quite ambiguous early in the analysis, before much is known about the details of the patient's unconscious fantasy life. Ultimately, the gender of the analyst will not significantly interfere with the full development of a transference that expresses the patient's enduring unconscious wishes and conflicts, even though it may obscure recognition of some aspects through its influence on organization and manifest configuration of the transference, especially in the opening phase (Raphling and Chused, 1988).

Erotic transference became immediately prominent in each of the three clinical examples even though the genders of only one analyst/patient dyad (CW) duplicated the incestuous experience. The apparently homosexual transference of female patient AV to her female analyst seemed largely defensive against a revival of the traumatic father-daughter sexual relationship and the hostility of the patient toward both parental objects, although later in the analysis negative oedipal wishes expressed homosexuality more directly. Patient BD's erotic transference to her male analyst repeated the homosexual relationship with her mother in specific details reconstructed from evidence uncovered in her previous analysis with a woman; the transference was, however, consciously experienced by the patient as heterosexual early in the analysis, owing to the organizing influence of the analyst's actual gender. Patients BD and CW consciously experienced more intense sexual feelings and fantasies with their male analyst than they had previously with their female analysts. This sexual arousal seemed curiously true even for BD, whose childhood sexual experiences had been with her mother; nonetheless, the special impact of the homosexuality was still tempered by the reality of the analyst's gender. Patient AV, whose father had sexually abused her, was less occupied with conscious sexual thoughts and feelings about her female analyst. The analyst inferred from disguised derivative material that preoedipal maternal transference manifestations were tinged with homosexuality, although an awareness of the sexual transference, which had to cross gender lines, was obscured by an emphasis on the analyst's actual gender.

The derivatives of a childhood seduction seem to be most directly and explicitly expressed and experienced as sexual in the here and now of transference repetition when the analyst's gender is the same as the object around which the patient's sexuality is predominantly organized, even when the gender of this conscious object choice is not the same as that of the seducing parent. When the analyst's gender is not the same as that of the patient's primary sexual object choice, the revival of incestuous experience in transference seems less obviously sexual. Thus, the heterosexual patient BD's transference, containing references to incestuous experience, was more overtly erotic with her male analyst than with her female analyst even though her incestuous object was her mother.

Patients who have been sexually abused are disposed to erotize erotic transference and analysis generally (Blum, 1973). They view analysis as a seduction and test out their expectation that sexual wishes will be actualized within the analysis. The erotic transference is frequently expressed as repetitive enactments of the original incestuous experience. For abused patients, erotization is preferable to the threat of loss of love or object loss. Patients' needs to gauge their vulnerability to the analyst while measuring and exercising their power over him gains expression in the erotized transference. These enactments and erotization of the analysis are attempts at mastery through action. They test the boundary between trial action in thought and irrevocable action in deed. Whether erotic transference is acted out as an identification with the seducing parent or as the victim in a masochistic revival of the incestuous experience, attempts at mastery through action constantly pressure the analyst to abandon neutral inquiry and abstinence for countertransference enactment.

Erotization also defends against an upsurge of aggression as hostile impulses are disguised by the manifest sexuality of incestuous enactments. The defensive posture of identification with the aggressor is transformed in transference revivals of the incestuous experience to an expression of retaliation and revenge.

A patient's seductive attempts to actualize the incestuous experience may succeed in drawing the analyst into unavoidable countertransference enactments surprisingly early in the analysis, when the therapeutic alliance is less sure and transference material ill understood. The patient is still very much a mystery to the analyst.

This lack of knowledge about the patient is, of course, inherent in the opening phase and promotes the analyst's vulnerability to countertransference enactments. In all three clinical examples, the patients manifested obvious (at least to the analyst) erotic transferences early in the opening phase. The analyst's usual role-responsiveness (Sandler, 1976) to the pressures of transference was transiently carried into action with patients AV and BD. Patient AV's analyst became aware of her susceptibility to AV's seductive appeal. The patient's enactments in the opening phase made the analysis an exciting sexual game, which continued to press its claim on the analyst's neutrality despite self-analytic clarification of countertransference and counteridentification. The analyst's wish not to have her standard technique become part of the patient's seductive enactments and perceptions had to be balanced against collusion with the patient in the mutual temptation to ignore the erotic influence on the analytic work and accept uncritically the patient's attempts to replace her perception of the analyst as a dangerous sexual object with an equally unrealistic one as totally benign and nonsexual. Such a collusion would have replicated the need of patient and parents alike to deny the incestuous nature of their relationship and would have reinforced the patient's pathological distortion of reality. An outward appearance of neutrality can easily be a countertransference enactment that masks the loss of a truly neutral inquiring stance (Jacobs, 1986). The analyst's continuing effort to maintain her neutrality mirrored the patient's constant inner struggle with the wished for but prohibited incestuous seduction. The analyst's complementary struggle provided an immediacy of experience that enhanced and authenticated understanding of her patient's conflicts.

Patient BD's pervasive erotization of the analytic situation was a core issue of the opening phase. She was uncertain about which of the participants, patient or analyst, was erotizing the analysis. The countertransference enactment of staring at the patient gave to her projection a kernel of truth, which made the interpretation of her own conflicted seductive motives seem less convincing, highlighting the confusing split images of being the seducer or the seduced: the guilty or innocent one.

The occurrence of a traumatic event in the life of sexually abused patients may create a potential resistance to analysis in several important ways. The inescapable reality of incest and the external source of the trauma divert the patients' attention from their own instinctual wishes and unconscious fantasies. The patients' emotional attachment to indelible images of the traumatic event and abusing parents can lead to a habitual, pathological defensive posture favoring externalization, denial, and projection, which distort their reality and object relations. The emphasis on past reality increases resistance to understanding the role of their own fantasy elaborations in the production of trauma. Their exploration of intrapsychic conflict, the opportunity to obtain a better understanding of how the mind operates, is blocked. Their conviction about the experience in the here and now of transference manifestations and resistance is diminished. Similarly, the analyst's attention may be drawn away from analyzing intrapsychic conflict and transference. Patient AV's recounting of her conscious memories of incest drew her attention (and her analyst's) away from greater awareness of early transference manifestations, including the seductive transference of relating intriguing details of her unusual childhood sexual experiences.

If, however, the analyst does not sufficiently address the reality of the incest trauma, it may seem as if the analyst is colluding with patients in a denial of the event and its significance. Patients may not be able to acknowledge their own role in a forbidden act if it is treated by the analyst as an incestuous fantasy. Patients easily engage in a "conspiracy of silence" (Blum, 1985) with their analysts, thus repeating the dissimulation, distortion, and evasion associated with the original incestuous experiences.

Patient CW's realization that she may have suffered incest trauma occurred only after the analysis was well underway. The analytic work of the introductory phase enabled her to overcome a sense of shame and guilt sufficiently to reveal her suspicion that incest had actually occurred. The patient was compelled to remain silent about her incestuous experience, in effect, as a lifelong response to internal prohibitions and parental demands for secrecy. For much of the opening phase, her wish to confess and understand was balanced against her fear of punishment.

Early in the analysis, if the actual occurrence of incest is suspected but not certain, patient and analyst are unavoidably drawn into questioning whether the incest was a real experience or a fantasy. Both lose sight of the psychic reality when they search obsessively for verification of an actual traumatic event.

Patients who have suffered sexual abuse believe they are the exceptions (Kramer, 1987) and enter analysis expecting reparation from the analyst as compensation for traumatic suffering. This expectation can become a formidable resistance if it represents the only type of cure acceptable to the patient. As victims, these patients believe they are entitled to special treatment: gratification of forbidden wishes, with exemption from anxiety and guilt. The status as a victim of child abuse can from the onset of treatment also prove to be a resistance by disguising paradoxical feelings of narcissistic power and triumph. Though these patients have paid the price of being sexually abused, they are also exceptions to the universal prohibition against incest and have won a kind of pyrrhic oedipal victory.

The "special" appeal of a victimized patient can easily draw the analyst into countertransference enactments. Gabbard (1986) reported a case in which an experienced analyst deviated from ordinary technique from the very beginning of therapy to treat his patient as an exception. This special treatment was his counterresponse to her acting out an appeal to repeat the incestuous relationship she had had with her father. Incest, though ultimately abusive, had provided a kind of affection, something she had been deprived of by a rejecting mother. The analyst made the patient an exception in his effort not to be identified with the depriving mother.

Patients inevitably begin analysis with preconceived unconscious theories of pathogenesis and cure (Abend, 1979). Patients who have been traumatized by incestuous experience are likely to have a theory of cure in which psychoanalysis is an antidote to the sexual abuse they have suffered. Patients like AW and BD imagine that the best treatment is replacement of the abusing parent with an idealized loving and caring analyst/parent, who will provide a corrective emotional experience. What is more, they expect the analyst to gratify all their forbidden wishes. This expectation gains power in their minds from a sense of entitlement, rationalized as proper compensation due them for having endured a traumatic childhood. Such theories reinforce their reluctance to examine the contribution to their plight of their own sexual and aggressive wishes, superego pressures, and pathological defenses. Their self-image as the hapless victim is perpetuated as the reparation expected from analysis becomes a vindication and is seen as a proof of innocence. These patients are capable of clinging tenaciously throughout the analysis to their convictions about pathogenesis and expectations of cure unless those beliefs are recognized, explored, and thoroughly analyzed.

REFERENCES

Abend, S. (1979), Unconscious fantasy and theories of cure. *J. Amer. Psychoanal. Assn.*, 27:579–596.

Blum, H. (1973), Erotized transference. *J. Amer. Psychoanal. Assn.*, 21:61–76.

_____ (1985), Superego formation, adolescent transformation, and the adult neurosis. *J. Amer. Psychoanal. Assn.*, 33:887–909.

Brenner, C. (1979), Working alliance, therapeutic alliance, and transference. *J. Amer. Psychoanal. Assn.*, 27 Sup.: 137–158.

Gabbard, G. (1986), The special hospital patient. *Internat. Rev. Psycho-Anal.*, 13:333–347.

Jacobs, T. (1986), Countertransference enactments. *J. Amer. Psychoanal. Assn.*, 34:289–308.

Katan, A. (1973), Children who were raped. *The Psychoanalytic Study of the Child*, 28:208–224. New Haven, CT: Yale University Press.

Kramer, S. (1983), Object-coercive doubting: A pathological defense response to maternal incest. In: *Defense and Resistance*, ed. H. Blum. New York: International Universities Press, pp. 325–362.

_____ (1987), A contribution to the concept of "the exception" as a developmental phenomenon. *Child Abuse & Neglect*, 11:367–370.

Panel (1989), The opening phase of psychoanalysis. E.L. Auchincloss, reporter. *J. Amer. Psychoanal. Assn.*, 37:199–214.

Raphling, D. & Chused, J. (1988), Transference across gender lines, *J. Amer. Psychoanal. Assn.*, 36:77–104.

Rascovsky, M. & Rascovsky, A. (1950), On consummated incest. *Internat. J. Psycho-Anal.*, 31:42–48.

Sandler, J. (1976), Countertransference and role-responsiveness. *Internat. Rev. Psycho-Anal.*, 3:43–47.

Shengold, L. (1980), Some reflections on a case of mother/adolescent incest. *Internat. J. Psycho-Anal.*, 61:461–476.

Steele, B. (1986), Child abuse. In: *The Reconstruction of Trauma*, ed. A. Rothstein. Madison, CT: International Universities Press, pp. 59–72.

Stein, M. H. (1981). The unobjectionable part of the transference. *J. Amer. Psychoanal. Assn.*, 29:968–992.

5

The Impact of Incest Trauma on Ego Development

Anne E. Bernstein

When Freud (1894, 1895) began to study patients with hysterical symptoms, he repeatedly encountered stories of childhood sexual seduction. These led him to postulate that he had found *the* traumatic event at the root of adult hysterical symptom formation (Freud, 1896, 1905). Later, Freud (1909) began to question whether his patients had real memories of seduction or if these were fantasies. Although he ultimately abandoned his seduction hypothesis for a more complex model of neurosogenesis, Freud subsequently made several observations that indicated to him that tales of seduction might not be merely fantasy: "Phantasies of being seduced are of particular interest because so often they are not phantasies but real memories" (Freud, 1916–1917, p. 37); "Actual seduction is common enough" Freud (1931, p. 232). "The object of sexual seduction may direct her later sexual life so as to provoke entirely similar acts" Freud (1937, p. 75–76).

Schimek (1987) has reviewed in exquisite detail the vicissitudes of Freud's thinking about seduction. He weighed the difference between Freud's initial belief that seduction was real

Sections of this paper were published in Bernstein, A.E. (1989). Analysis of two adult female patients who had been victims of incest in childhood. *J. Amer. Acad. Psychoanal* 17: 207–212, 1989.

and his subsequent view that it was imagined and concluded that in Freud's patients the "crucial early past is not recollected but inferred and reconstructed as individual variations on a small number of universal themes and scenarios" (p. 964).

In contrast to Schimek's conclusions about Freud's early cases, my own clinical experience has been that memories of actual childhood seduction can be recalled in analysis. When reports of such memories are accompanied by specific ego deficits, panic states, traumatic dreams, or depersonalization, the clinician should be alerted to the possibility that the patient was a victim of actual incest trauma.

A BRIEF REVIEW OF THE LITERATURE

Commonly noted alterations in the ego in patients who have experienced incest trauma include cognitive deficits; difficulties in comprehension, attention, concentration, and memory; confusion; somatization; difficulty establishing basic trust; and use of the defense of vertical splitting (Burland and Raskin, Steele, both this volume). Fleiss (1973) noted, in addition, depressive affect and faulty regulation of self-esteem as the result of identification with the hated object and the patient's taking his or her ego as the object of aggression. Shengold (1963), however, ascribed depressive affect to the incorporation of the abusive parent into the superego, as well as into the ego. In reference to self-esteem, he believes that the perception of ugliness of the self is a projection of the perception of the mother's ugliness or the consequence of having felt ugly in the mother's eyes. Shengold (1974) and Kestenberg (1988) have postulated similar dynamics in adults who were holocaust victims in childhood and who felt empty, dead, or "like nothing."

In addition to the cognitive deficits already noted, Bender and Blau (1937) documented the impairment of the intellectual performance in 16 children who were victims of incest; their I.Q. had been established by formal psychological testing. For only one child could they clinically establish for the impairment a reason unrelated to the incest.

Katan (1973) mentioned the existence of a resistance to taking in, to making a whole out of fragments. That is, the intellectual synthetic function of the ego is impaired. Shengold (1979) noted that vertical splitting is a defense used to cope with overstimulation, thus compromising thinking and registration of events.

Ganzarain and Buchele (1988) highlighted the role played by the secret of the seduction in compromising the ability of the latency age child to participate in the peer group. Having missed the stage of affiliation with peers not only in latency but in adolescence, these patients are often socially isolated. They have therefore proposed group therapy as an adjunct to analysis or psychoanalytic psychotherapy. Blos (1965), writing about normal male prepubertal and early adolescent development, discussed the role played by adolescent friendships in detaching object cathexis from the oedipal father. He noted that the failure to detach object cathexis from the oedipal father results in the failure of consolidation of the ego ideal. Thus, the inability "to have buddies," proscribed by the "secret of incest," results in two further ego deficits—one within the ego ideal and the other in the negotiation of object relationships. Writing about female incest victims, O'Brien (1987) noted the same phenomenon. In addition, he comments on the propensity in these patients to early and excessive sexual activity.

Different alterations of the ego have been reported in patients who were participants in mother–son incest. Margolis (1977a) and Shengold (1980) provide examples of the "King of the World" phantasy that narcissistically inflates the self-representation of male patients who in reality achieved oedipal triumph. The infrequency of reports of consummated mother--son incest has itself been the subject of speculation. Wahl (1960) believed that the son-partner in mother–son incest is almost always psychotic. Thus, the son would be an unlikely subject for analysis. Another possibility raised by Shengold (1980) is that most psychiatrists are male and have a deep resistance to uncovering the fulfillment of the male's characteristic oedipal wish. He noted both his own resistance to telling colleagues about his paper as he wrote it and theirs to discussing it with him. When the discussion was joined, there was invariably a rapid shift to talking about father–daughter incest. In his opinion, a special forbiddenness centers on the wish to impregnate the mother.

It is worth noting the effects on the ego and the countertransference in mother–son incest, because they may lead us to consider the possibility of incest where we might otherwise not suspect it. As noted earlier, Margolis (1977 p. 276) described his patient as feeling as though he were "King of the World" after he had subdued and had intercourse with his mother. Shengold (1980) described his patient as arrogant and breezy and having a "let others wait for me" attitude. The patient's wife had to remind him that he was not royalty. This patient was described as having an almost delusional pride.

The second trait noted by Shengold was an aesthetic transmutation of the entire incestuous contact. Shengold's patient painted from memory an unforgettable picture full of sensory and sensual details. The memory was recalled in a soft focus and suffused with an aesthetic glow. His patient had had a lifelong intense feeling for beauty in nature and art.

Comparable self-inflation, "Queen of the World" fantasies, entitlement, and artistic sensibility are not reported to be legacies of father–daughter incest. Maternal deprivation is seen in incest victims of both sexes (Rascovsky and Rascovsky, 1950).

In the sections that follow, I present case material from the psychoanalytic treatment of two adult female patients, including an analytic hour that occurred late in the second analysis. The case material illustrates the ego deformations/alterations that occur in female patients who have experienced incest trauma. In particular, I pay careful attention to the way some of the ego developmental issues colored both the transference and the countertransference in the course of the analyses.

CASE EXAMPLES

Mrs. A

Mrs. A, was a 32-year-old married mother of three children, a homemaker. She sought treatment for the third time because of depression, feelings that she was dead or in a fog, an inability to think or concentrate, and hypersomnolence. In addition, she had gained 70 pounds, much to the dismay of her family. Her husband no longer found her sexually attractive, and she was unwilling to undress in front of him because she was ashamed of her body, thereby precluding sexual activity. When first evaluated for treatment, she was motorically retarded and hardly coherent. Psychotherapy and a series of antidepressant medications produced little response. A psychological test battery obtained at that time and available to me when I first saw her noted that she might have been an incest victim. I unconsciously chose to deny that information. The patient was recovering from her psychomotor retardation and wanted to talk. She requested several sessions a week and provided the following history, supplemented here with other data.

She was the older of two siblings of a businessman and housewife. Her brother, two years her junior, was born with clubbed feet, and she was much involved in his early care. She described her mother as a self-centered and shallow woman who kept candy locked away from the children, but that she herself would sit in bed and eat. The family always had household help to take care of the children. Her mother had a long list of "questions we don't ask," including "What is for dinner?" Mrs. A described her father as the parent involved with her school work, who took her ice skating and encouraged her in a variety of activities, including piano lessons. She remembered that when she was about nine years old he became irrascible, often chasing her around the house and beating her. She told him to "drop dead." She stubbornly would never give in. She carried this stubbornness to school, where she functioned well. When she was 11, her father was admitted to the hospital for what she was vaguely told was an operation. She remembered going in to visit him and wondering why he did not recognize her. He returned home with his head swathed in bandages and was confined to bed. That summer she was sent to camp and returned to live with her aunt, from whose home she went to school.

On her birthday, her mother made her a small party, handed her her gift, and then told her that her father had died. She was not permitted to go to the funeral but was allowed to stay home from school for a day. Her mother had answered few questions about her father's death except to say that he had had brain cancer and that he had gone down hill rapidly from his first symptom—"sensing a strange odor"—to his surgery and death.

Mrs. A felt that with her father's death she had "lost everything, both mother and father." Her father had taken on many maternal functions during her childhood. After his death, her mother's family, fearing that Mrs. A's mother might have a nervous breakdown, whisked mother off on a grand tour of Europe. After mother's return, the patient and her brother continued to live with their aunt. Mrs. A continued to do well in school, and was very popular, for another year and a half, when at age 14 suddenly everything "fell apart." She resigned from the sports teams, her grades slipped, and she became reclusive. She did, however, manage to attend college, although she still lived at home with her mother. She met her husband, who lived in her apartment building, while she was walking the family dog. While they were courting, they had intercourse in mother's living room while mother was in the house.

Mrs. A seemed insatiable to her husband, who never forgave her for her sexual demands. She knew on her honeymoon that "something was wrong," but he reassured her that this was not so. In the early years of the marriage, he was building a business and often was away from home while she stayed home to raise her children. After the birth of her third child, her second daughter, she had a postpartum depression and could not be left alone because she was suicidal. She recovered and continued to devote herself to raising her children. Aside from playing the piano she did little else. Meanwhile, her husband became sexually involved with his secretary, whom he had been maintaining in an apartment for a year. He left the patient but was forced to return to her by his parents. Asked how he could have had an affair for so long without her knowledge, she initially replied, "In my home, we were trained not to see what we saw nor hear what we heard." For years, she was unable to elaborate on this statement.

Despite Mrs. A's obvious deficits and because of her history of ego strengths, which seemed to have been strangely and suddenly lost during adolescence, I offered her psychoanalysis. She readily agreed, stating that there was something terribly wrong with her and that analysis was her last hope. She said that for the first time in several years she occasionally had an idea but didn't know where it came from. By this she meant that she could think about solving simple problems like scheduling, could not figure them out, and then an idea would come to her "out of nowhere." These idea felt at once obvious and comfortable, yet she had no control over when they would occur to her or "where she had gotten them." It seemed to me that she had split off her controlled, deliberate cognitive functioning, along with whatever was being repressed. We were, in fact, to learn that there was a portion of her mind that she did not feel she owned.

We spent the first year of her analysis talking about everyday events and problems. She verbalized easily and with the kind of confidentiality that reminded me of adolescent girl-talk. She complained obsessionally about feeling very blank, empty, and dead outside of our sessions.

Yet, she began to exercise and diet and lost the 70 lbs she had gained. She said that she could not guarantee that she would keep this up. This positive behavior, which she wanted desperately to sustain, seemed very unreliable and undependable to her.

One annoying "depressive symptom" remained. She would wake up early in the morning, fall asleep, reawaken, and repeat this pattern for hours. She was unable to get out of bed except on those days that she had to drive her children to school. She had only one friend and confidant, a neighbor who had invited her to join in her business, which she did for a short while.

She also began to become angry because her husband expected her to wait on him but was never available to her or the children. She wondered if he was having another affair and began to remember evidence that indeed he had been unfaithful almost all of their married life. She recalled that she could never confront him, or consider leaving him, because she had no one in her corner. Her father had always "been in her corner" when she was a child. Her transference was that of a child with a supportive parent. She began to acknowledge her husband's promiscuous behavior. She even confronted him with clear evidence, which he denied. She was unhappy and spent much of her analytic time marshaling evidence of his wrongdoing to present to me. She and her husband finally separated, and he immediately moved in with a divorced neighbor with whom he had been having an affair. Their subsequent divorce negotiations were long and difficult, as were her relationships with her children during this period. She proceeded doggedly to "clear up her life," which she did, despite her cognitive limitations, in order to get back to her analysis. She wanted to explore the problem of why she could not remember, or figure out, so many things in her life. She began to spend a couple of hours a day sitting in a chair and putting herself into a semitrance state in which, with a great deal of anxiety and some depersonalization, she remembered bits and pieces of her childhood. When I interpreted that she was trying to do her analysis without me, she suddenly recalled a story that she had been told about herself as a child. She had begun talking very early and would adamantly refuse help, even in walking, saying, "I do it dyself [myself]." This was her way of rejecting a distant and "proper" nanny, a woman was hired by her mother, who wanted nothing to do with, or for, the patient.

Mrs. A's early dreams were fractured fragments that proved unanalyzable. Now she had a full dream. Her father's head was slowly getting bigger and bigger until it finally burst. Associations led to the reconstruction that his illness must have evolved slowly rather than suddenly. This reconstruction later proved correct, but it touched on only one meaning of the dream. Mrs. A panicked, depersonalized, and felt that she was suddenly blind. She needed to be blind to the sexual meaning of the dream and was unconscious of this need. The panic manifestly related to the fact that her father had not recognized her after his return from the hospital because he was neurologically blind.

She spent a great many hours piecing together the fact that her father's erratic behavior—chasing her, hitting her—was the result of his slowly growing tumor. During this time she was able to recover memories of many ordinary events of her childhood. There seemed to be no reason why names of girlfriends, the patient's path to school, or simple school activities should have been split off. Split they were and not repressed. In the patient's words, "I always knew about that, only, I never thought about it. If I ever wanted to, like when my children were in plays or started a new subject, it just wasn't there. I couldn't think. It wasn't like forgetting. Once in a while, I'd have a flash, the color of a dress I'd worn, but then I couldn't be sure whether it was real or made up." She had no other thoughts about this.

Then she brought a dream in which she visualized the details of her childhood bedroom—the piano, the bed, chair, the window shades. She said that this dream was a strange one, because of the angle from which she was looking. I remarked that from her description it must have been early morning. She must have been lying face down with her neck craned up. She answered immediately, "Yes, that's when he used to do it to me" and burst into tears.

Subsequently she gave a history of her father's intercourse with her during the onset of his illness. She had been between nine and eleven years old. At this point in her analysis, she had trouble eating reasonably and was substituting a very sweet ice cream, eaten by the quart, for meals. She fantasied that this was "mother's milk." She also developed Raynaud's Syndrome, "cold feet," which interfered with her running exercise. As the panic subsided, she entered a period of severe mourning. She felt that her father had been everything to her—caretaker, mentor, and lover. She realized that she had encouraged this relationship, rationalizing that it was necessary because her mother had been so uncaring. She developed very loving positive feelings about me, and I became the idealized father of her early childhood.

This transference paradigm shifted during my summer vacation. She saw me, in my absence, as the self-involved, abandoning mother. She became sexually reinvolved with her ex-husband, whom she saw symbolically as her father. She imagined that I would not care. For the first time since their courtship, she became openly seductive and sexually free. Her ex-husband, however, continued other sexual liaisons. She began a campaign to convince him that she was a better lover than his other paramours. She recalled "knowing" as a child that she would be a better wife for her father than her mother had been. She had fantasied being his wife.

She remembered that as an oedipal child, she would awaken at night and insist that her father come to soothe her. She developed the habit of demanding that he take her to the bathroom. Ostensibly because the floor was cold, she would stand on his feet facing him with her arms around him and he would walk her on his feet to the bathroom and back. She felt erotically aroused by this memory. She again mourned his loss. She told me that she needed to understand why she had done so well for almost two years after her father's death until the death of her beloved aunt, followed immediately by the death of her best friend's mother, who had served as a mother surrogate. She kissed this dead woman goodbye. She then left for a party with a boy to whom she was attracted, but had a sudden thought at the party, "My life is over now." This last loss and her emergent adolescent sexuality threatened her repression. She said she "died psychologically," which is the way she experienced her severe ego splitting.

She turned her attention to the present, exploring employment and the letting go of her children, to whom she had always tried to "be everything." The latter proved a very difficult issue. When I invited her to explore it, she recalled an episode of being hysterical and requiring acute psychiatric intervention when she learned that one of her daughters had engaged in sexual play with a cousin one year older. She insisted then that her daughter had been raped. At the time of the incident, her husband had reminded her of another incident, which had occurred when her older daughter was pubescent. Mrs. A had encouraged this girl to dress up in her mother's sheer nightgowns to await her father's evening arrival. Fortunately, the father recognized that he was becoming aroused and put a stop to the behavior.

The patient was unconscious, at the time, of the meaning of this reenactment. Now she was afraid of her children's emerging sexuality and of her own sexual needs. She began to masturbate with latency-appropriate "Prince Charming" fantasies. She revealed that during her marriage her fantasy during sexual relations was that her husband was "doing it to her against her will." For the first time she could make the connection to the incest without panic. Yet any time she made those connections, she would experience transient cognitive deficits in other areas.

As she began to date, she hid the details from me, much as she had hidden the incest from her mother. I interpreted this aspect of the maternal transference. She was secretive about successes and complained about feeling depressed, although she did not appear clinically depressed. She was afraid that her business success, her new friendships, and resolving cognitive abilities would cause me to abandon her. She wanted a real relationship with me, and I interpreted her need for a good mother. Her mother was still a self-centered, cold, and reclusive woman. Her own attractiveness and willingness to be helpful caused her sister-in-law and then women business associates to adopt a supportive and mentoring role toward her. Although her former husband behaved very badly toward their children, she insisted that her divorce had been a mistake and was rejecting and demeaning of her suitors. No one was good enough. Her quest for an idealized father was repeatedly interpreted but with little effect. She continued to date but terminated analysis still unwilling to settle for anyone who fell short of her idealization.

Pivotal points of this long analysis have been chosen to illustrate the patient's depressive affect, defective sense of ownership of the self, severe cognitive deficits due to splitting, doubting of reality, cognitive confusion, panic and depersonalization with recovery of the incest experience, defensive somatization, a reworking of the need for a close peer relationship, and, finally, the need for a real relationship with the analyst as a good mother.

Mrs. L

Mrs. L was a married business executive. She had begun a previous analysis during her mother's terminal illness, when marital problems produced her first work difficulties, leading to several job changes. She never felt comfortable with her male analyst, who had allegedly dealt with her "penis envy." This treatment failed to improve either her work adjustment or her failing marriage. Her husband's therapist subsequently referred her to me. The patient presented herself to me with the complaint that she thought she ought to have a child before reaching the end of her childbearing years, despite having neither a desire for a child nor any maternal feelings toward the children of others. She believed she had never resolved her relationship with her mother and reported that she first became aware of emotional problems after a fight with her mother, in which she attempted to limit mother's intrusion into her life. Following the fight, mother had had a cerebrovascular accident, from which she never fully recovered. Mrs. L's father blamed her for her mother's progressive invalidism and death. Mrs. L said that she had not felt guilty but had suffered depression, a severe loss of self-esteem, frightening episodes of panic, and depersonalization states in which she felt that her "head was expanding." She also had irritable bowel syndrome and recurrent nonspecific vaginitis.

Her work with me initially centered on her relationship with her mother. Her birth had caused her domineering European father to demand that mother give up her employment and remain at home, despite the fact that the family had many servants. The patient perceived her mother as the neutral parent in contrast to her father, who was alternately critical and unavailable. He is alleged to have wanted a son. The patient's primary relationships in childhood were with household pets and later with her horse. She often withdrew into a fantasy world of lush visual imagery, which she later applied successfully to her work. Her initial transference was withholding, cold, and aloof, although she did not experience herself this way. She was always polite and correct, but lacked warmth or trust. Analysis of this transference led to feelings that her mother had criticized, neutered, and neutralized her.

Eventually, the patient, who had never felt pretty, abandoned her business suits for attractive feminine clothing. Her vaginitis flared. During one session, I noted that she seemed to be trying to hide her hands from me. She revealed that she had had her first manicure and had fantasied my (her mother's) competitive disapproval. Her hiding her hands had another basis. She recalled her closeness to father—their sailing together, his pride in her ability with horses, his driving her to the riding stable. She had showered with him until age five, when she impulsively reached up and pulled on his penis. With this report, her immediate associations shifted to a period of militant feminism early in her career, which made her feel more respected and competent, as if she had a penis. She was becoming more comfortable and confident of her growing femininity. She began to write a book that had in it a fierce looking animal, later analyzed as a symbol for her mother. Episodes of dissociation occurred as she wrote. She linked these with a feeling of being disconnected from the analyst. As she became more in touch with her rage toward her mother and me, she became less angry at her husband. After two years of analysis she became emotionally involved with the children of her friends and felt ready to begin a pregnancy.

Then her father became critically ill and rebuffed her attempts at reconciliation. She dreamed of herself as a painted Easter egg sitting silently at her parents' table, an object there to amuse and gratify them. She again recalled her father's pride in, and encouragement of, her athletic activities. She recalled playing with him as a child. She remembered a traumatic episode during her early adolescence when she had acquiesced to penetration from behind by a household workman. She confessed this to a favorite aunt with whom she felt very close, only to be "betrayed" by having the aunt tell the story to her parents, who called the police. The fantasy of anal penetration became her obligatory masturbation fantasy, for reasons she did not understand.

Now she wanted desperately to become pregnant, but her husband refused, and she became angry and irritable with him. He was emotionally unsupportive, violent, erratic, and financially dependent on the patient. He never paid his bills on time, received numerous speeding tickets, and drove after his license was revoked. After my vacation, she returned with a dream. "I was a boy. Someone called a lady, you, to take care of me. The lady already had other kids to look after. She said that I could come but she might not be able to pay much attention to me." She was able to associatively link this with her perceived abandonment by the mother/analyst and the husband's thwarting her wish to become pregnant. In this context she regressed to a masculine identification, repeating her pattern of returning to her father when mother was unavailable.

Eventually, she ended her marriage. After a while, she was

again able to work successfully and made plans to enjoy her life. However, a long, fluctuating series of physical complaints seemed always to obstruct her. She had intractable headaches, which she called "migraines," blurred vision, gastrointestinal problems, recurrent urinary tract complaints, recurrent vaginal candidiasis, and frequent untoward reactions to medications given for these conditions.

She told me that these symptoms must relate to something as yet undiscovered in her analysis, which was then in its fourth year. Subsequently, she dreamed of sailing in a boat, with a man looming over her. Her first association was to her father and then to a peculiar episode of derealization and depersonalization that has occurred in my office years before and that she had failed to report. She recalled feeling as if the walls were closing in on her and that my white desk looked like a sail.

Following the dream, and noting that I looked sad, she recovered important memories. These concerned the family's summer home, where she and mother had stayed during the week while her father remained in the city. At that time, when the patient was in early latency, her mother was very depressed and isolated from her daughter. My patient became involved in sexual play (on a boat) with a neighbor's little boy. The sexual play resulted in the loss of her friends, who ostracized her. In the transference, my patient remained superficially polite but affectively aloof from me. She was aware through interpretation that she was treating me the way her mother had treated her. Only when she developed painful hemorrhoids requiring surgery and felt surprised and grateful that I raised the issue of her anxiety over the surgery and her fears about it, did she experience any warmth toward me. At home, when she was ill, she had been shunted to one or another Nannie. She had a series of dreams that seemed to refer to anal intercourse. For example, she dreamed that she had had sex and was left with "shit and blood" all over her. I asked about whether she had in fact had had anal intercourse. She panicked—felt her body getting smaller, a crushing pain in her chest, and the walls of my office closing in around her. So great was her panic that, gasping for breath, she fled from the consultation room to the waiting room. I followed to ask if she was all right. She felt faint, did not feel she could return to the session, but asked if she could sit in the waiting room until she could compose herself. I told her she could. In the subsequent hours, she did not directly refer to this departure from standard procedure. However, I believe that it partially contributed to a structural change in her ego, a change that involved the incorporation of me as a responsive, concerned, and empathic object and led to an increased capacity for trust.

The following material emerged in bits and pieces of visual and olfactory images. She remembered the smell of alcohol, her childhood bedroom, a man who had attacked her, and going to the bathroom to clean herself of blood and feces. She initially connected the smell of alcohol with her father and then remembered that a man had come into her bed. She had the sensation of not being able to breathe, of feeling crushed by a weight across her chest, and of her father saying that he wouldn't hurt her. An X-ray taken when she was an adult disclosed an old, healed fracture of her clavicle. Its origin was uncertain. Thus emerged the data for our reconstruction of father's sexual abuse.

With great shame, she remembered throwing her cats against the walls. I asked where her mother had been during the incestuous attacks. She was amazed that she had never told me that her mother was an alcoholic who often drank herself sick or into a stupor. I interjected my suspicion that perhaps mother had abused her when she was a young child, throwing her against the wall as she did later with her cats. She remembered. She had turned to her father for mothering, as well as for satisfaction of her oedipal desires. It was this fusion of dependent needs and sexual excitement that she had reenacted with the little boy on the boat when her mother was depressed.

As this material was uncovered, memories of her mother were also recalled. (Her father had died several years before, followed soon by her favorite aunt, her mother's sister.) Aside from this aunt, the patient knew nothing of her mother's family nor their history. A series of dreams about going to temple on the Jewish holidays, which indeed she had done in the past with a Jewish friend, led to fantasies about my religion and queries about it. These were the first inquiries about my personal life. In the past when I was absent for Jewish holidays she did not question or comment. Just as I began to wonder whether her mother was

Jewish and estranged from her family, she had the same suspicion. She arranged a visit with a paternal cousin from another city who comfirmed that her mother was indeed Jewish.

Mrs. L now saw herself as one who had suffered terribly, and she actively decided to make plans to start anew and enjoy life. She bought herself a horse but feared telling me about it, dreading my jealousy. She dreamed that rivers and stones and fences interfered with her riding. I remarked that she seemed to be putting obstacles in her own path. She fantasied that if she was successful, I would terminate her treatment, abandoning her as her mother had. Shortly thereafter she injured her back seriously by overdoing driving and riding and became furious at me for "predicting" her failure. Further work had to be done on the raging negative transference. She said that she had always hated my jewelry and recalled that mother had worn a great deal of jewelry given to her by father. She said, "She got the jewelry and I got screwed in the ass." She recalled the work problems that had occurred during her mother's illness prior to her first analysis. She realized that she had not been able to negotiate at work because she always felt she would "get it in the ass." This insight clarified why she had had such difficulty in negotiating work-necessitated changes of analytic hours, preferring instead to skip an occasional session and pay for it. Recollections of her parents were still accompanied by panic and rage, but the depersonalization stopped as her rage in the maternal transference was analyzed. It was then possible to analyze the "expanding head" symptom as an identification with her father's erect penis. She said a dream about cutting her cat's claws about letting herself be declawed, letting her defenses down. Subsequently she began to meet men with whom there was a chance of intimacy. She realized that she had always been afraid of maternal men. In addition, she began to treat me as the good aunt with whom she could share delicious morsels of these relationships.

Years later, after much working through took place around these issues, the following session occurred:

Mrs. A buzzed the outside door unusually (10 minutes) early and announced, "It's *your* early bird." On the way in she remarked that she had never before seen me as doing anything but a job, albeit in a benevolent manner. When she lay on the couch, she told me that she had had a nightmare that morning but that she had to remember to talk about sex with J, her current lover. She grimaced and said, "You know how much I love to talk about that." Again uncharacteristically, she had written this dream down. She continued. "You know how often I do that, once every three years, but I couldn't seem to get out of the dream."

"I was on a small boat, the kind I used to sail on with my father. Wait, I first remembered an earlier dream. It took place by the water, old rotted docks, like at M [where the family had had a summer cottage]. J and I were together; we might have been married. There were bullets, like a war, maybe a Vietnam scene. Oh yes, I've been hearing about the movie, 'Platoon,' that is getting all those awards. We were escaping, holding hands, running to the edge of the dock, but I wasn't afraid. I felt that I would be safe with him. That was not a nightmare. I told it first because it was an earlier dream.

"The nightmare was on a small boat. I was very preoccupied with coiling the lines. My father had an obsession about not letting the lines loose, so that they could get all fouled up when you needed them. People always laugh at me. I'm the one who walks around fixing up the lines. I was fixing up the lines and checking the safety gear, the life preservers—no the lifejackets. They were in a cabinet with the foul-weather gear. Then the man overboard line, as I was figuring what length I would need, the boat suddenly began to get bigger and bigger, higher out of the water. I needed a longer and longer line. The water kept getting lower and lower as if I were on a yacht, then an ocean liner. I was panicked even when I woke up; I couldn't get out of the dream. That's such a funny thing about the lines. Some people wrap the lines around and around the cleats—that's ugly [she shuddered], and it's not safe. You can't get them loose if you need them in a hurry. I always coil the lines beside the cleats. I have a sudden picture of a cleat sticking up with the lines around and around it. I really can't stand that; strange to have such strong feelings as I picture it. Now I have to talk about J."

She spoke in great detail about their social activities, the first two weeks she had been with him, and how sexually excited she had felt—all the time "hot to trot." The first couple of times they made love, she could not have an orgasm. At first she felt that it was because she had strained her back several months ago and it was still sometimes painful when her muscles tensed. By the third time they had made love, she thought she was inorgasmic because her defenses were down. This was really the first time she had allowed herself to have a tender and loving relationship. She mentioned her anorgasmia to J, and he dismissed it, saying, "Don't worry about it." She felt enraged that he did not care about her need to find release. She knew that the rage was irrational, because he was very considerate and was probably trying to reassure her not to worry, that it would happen eventually. Yet she felt enraged and could not get rid of the feeling. She did not want to spend as much time with J as he wanted to because she had many interests and many friends, yet sex was very exciting and she did not want to lose that. She was still unable to be orgasmic and wanted to work that out. She had the fantasy that if she suggested spending less time together, he would strangle her. Once, at the beginning of the relationship, when he had held her around the neck to bring her face close to his, she had panicked. She pushed him away and exclaimed, "Never do that again!" She wondered what the nightmare had to do with J.

I said that she had begun to talk about her association to sailing with her father and had gone on to talk about lovemaking with J. She said, "Something happened on that boat, too, but I felt safe with my father then. It was before the sodomy. He used to put his hands on mine and teach me how to tie the lines."

I asked, "Is that all he taught you to do with your hands?"

She gasped. "God, the lines around the cleat, my hands around his penis. That's why the boat got bigger and bigger and it was so scary—my hair is standing on end. I actually feel my hair standing on end. But something else happened about strangling—no that was in the bedroom—I know he held me down with his arm around my chest; I felt I couldn't breathe. But do you think he tried to strangle me? Wait, there's a part of the dream of my trying to put the lights on the boat—not when it was a little boat—I mean when it got yacht size. Did he try to strangle me then? No, it was in the bedroom. I have the same feeling now as I get in a small hot room. Like I can't breathe. Do you think he actually tried to strangle me? He couldn't have. That's just too awful. When does this ever end? Why should he try to kill me? Bombed out of your mind on alcohol. There's no telling what you might do, but why?"

"Did you try to put the lights on?" I asked.

She answered, "I must have struggled to do something like that. I wasn't just going to take all that pain. I must have struggled. I know I did, because my ass hurts right now. I went to Dr. J, who did my hemorrhoids. He told me that my ass was hanging down and he had to tack it up. I know you thought it was strange when I told it to you after the surgery. (I had asked her, "He did what?" at the time), but, she continued, he mentioned it again. It was a technical name something with 'S' lapse.' "

"Prolapse?" I asked (in another example of the countertransference wish to be a good and helpful mother).

"Yes, that's it. I wanted to ask him whether that could have been the result of sodomy, but I didn't ask. I know it could, because it happens in homosexuals, who really tear up their asses. I also found out that he had tied off two hemorrhoids that I knew about and also repaired two fissures. That's bad enough. I don't believe my father strangled me. My hair is standing on end now because I know it really happened. I can feel it. I am trying to stay controlled, but I feel hysterical." She sat up and said tremulously, her eyes filled with tears, "Do you know how bad I feel? Yes, you do. I know you do and that helps." I noted the change in the nature of the transference. Although she sat up and cried, she did not flee the consultation room.

DISCUSSION

Both patients I have described experienced incest trauma and remembered it in the course of long analyses. The memories emerged over time with severe panic and depersonalizations. Both patients had experienced maternal deprivation: Mrs. A because her mother was narcissistically preoccupied; Mrs. L., first because her mother was depressed and later because her mother became alcoholic and was often in a stupor. Both patients provoked countertransference reactions in me. Mrs. A's former therapist had presented me with psychological tests that raised the possibility of incest. Yet I chose to ignore this data and probably unconsciously colluded with Mrs. A in ignoring evidence that she had a secret. Mrs. L provoked the counter-transference need to be soothing, helpful, and protective.

Both patients dealt with the incest trauma by vertical splitting or compartmentalization. They learned not to trust their percep-tions of reality and to keep secrets. Mrs. A did not "see" what she saw or "hear" what she heard. This woman, who turned out to be naturally inquisitive, had failed to find out the real nature of her father's terminal illness.

Mrs. L hid behind the façade of a cultural reticence (she was a "typical Wasp") and never inquired about her mother's family or past history, even though she had an aunt, her mother's sister, to whom she spoke about everything. Both learned not to ask or be asked questions, thus ensuring their secret.

Mrs. A, who had experienced the incest as loving, if painful and shameful, had a poor capacity for peer relationships. She had married a man whom she expected to be everything to her, as her father had been. Her sexual relationship with her husband began under the sway of the repetition compulsion. She would force intercourse in the living room near her mother's bedroom and seemed insatiable. She herself was a loving mother, who nevertheless arranged for her daughter to be dressed seductively to greet her father in the evening. Again, we see the effects of the pressure to repeat her trauma.

Mrs. L had better, if superficial, peer relationships. She had married a controlling man with the potential to be physically violent. Although she was popular with children, she had no maternal wishes or desires.

If there is such a thing as "loving incest," Mrs. A, who had that experience, was nonetheless much more functionally im-paired than Mrs. L. She had a paralyzing depression, with massively impaired cognitive functioning in all areas. She could not attend, concentrate, or remember. She could not read a newspaper. She had trouble at the piano.

Mrs. L., on the other hand, the victim of anal rape, functioned at her job, read, managed finances, had hobbies carried over from childhood, and could furnish some accounting of her history of growing up. She had less doubt of reality, less generalized cognitive confusion, and a greater tendency to somatization. One symptom, the feeling that her head was getting larger, was linked to her defective sense of control over herself. Mrs. A experienced her cognitive impairment in much the same way. Mrs. L's swelling head represented an identification with her father's swelling penis.

Both patients suffered from depressive affect. For Mrs. A, that depression was primary and related to the loss of her father, reinforced by the successive loss of other love objects. It also represented the loss of being special, father's special girl. For Mrs. L, depression was secondary to the repeated attacks of depersonalization. Each of these women had impaired self-esteem. Mrs. A could not feel pretty. This phenomenon was secondary to maternal rejection by a very self-absorbed, competitive mother concerned with her own appearance. Mrs. L looked and felt masculine, both as a rejection of her depressed, alcoholic mother and in identification with her successful, aggressive father. In addition, she felt like "nothing," despite her career achievements. Anything she did accomplish was felt to be superficial. She felt empty inside, as seen in her dream of the painted egg. I believe that this perception of herself as empty defended against the perception of a sadistic object representation, her father, which became part of her self-representation.

Let us now consider the transferences as they unfolded and the effect that analysis had on the development and repair of these patients' egos.

Mrs. A spent the first year of her analysis as if resuming where she had left off in her adolescence—where adolescent girl-talk had ceased in the defense of her secret. She treated me as if I were an adolescent best friend. She exercised and dieted in ways that were reminiscent of the attempts of adolescent girls to shed baby fat and improve their physical appearance. She could not trust the constancy of her resolve and looked to me for the support and approval an adolescent might need from her peer group, before fully internalizing a self-image as an adult, with a new appearance that could be maintained. She briefly joined a neighbor's business, making a tentative foray into the world of adult gainful employment. Her sessions were filled with repetitious descriptions of the peculiar morning symptoms of early awakening and falling back to sleep. Then she complained about waiting on her husband and wondered about the possibility of his sexual life away from her. She was beginning to tell me symbolically about her life with her father. The theme of needing someone in her corner, as her father had been, entered the transference. She spent much of her analytic time marshaling evidence about her husband's (symbolically father's) infidelities. She saw me as someone (a good mother) who would listen and help her clear up her life. She negotiated a difficult divorce, temporarily overcoming her cognitive limitations.

During the next period she began analyzing herself outside of her analytic hours. When I interpreted this as an attempt at self-analysis, she presented her first early memory of being a very stubborn, self-sufficient child who got along without a mother. She interpreted my not interdicting her self-analysis as support for her independence. My perceived support allowed her to undo a defensive regression in which she had never before presented a full dream. She recovered a capacity for symbolization that had been split off and compartmentalized with her secret. The reconstruction of her father's slowly developing illness got close enough to the incest trauma to cause panic, depersonalization, and identification with her father's terminal symptom, blindness. She needed to be "blind" to the sexual meaning of the dream of her father's expanding head, as she needed to be blind to the incest trauma.

Many analytic hours were spent around her father's erratic behavior, which was the result of a slowly growing intracranial mass. The incest still remained split off. Its compartment, however, was getting smaller, as indicated by her beginning to recall school activities and friendships. Her repetitious statement, "I always knew that," was, of course, true. There was little to say or interpret. Hour after hour she would take up where she had left off, adding details that came in flashes and seemed strange to her. In the countertransference, I felt as if I were the loom on which she rewove the tapestry of her childhood. This was a seamless process, as if I provided the structure upon which cognition is built. In the transference, I was the mother of early childhood, who allows for and protects the coalescence of brief cognitive flashes into a richer and fuller picture of cognition. She then brought the breakthrough dream, which provided, with very little disguise, a picture of the physical setting of the incest. My interpretation of her physical position on the bed facilitated the recall of the incestuous events. She began binge-eating ice cream, which she aptly interpreted as "mother's milk." I only later realized that the ice cream binges were an attempt to replace me. She anticipated in the maternal transference that I would withdraw from her because she had usurped my (her mother's) place with her father. She entered a period of mourning for her father and transferred her positive, loving feelings for him to me.

A transference shift occurred during my vacation. I became the abandoning, selfish mother, and she resumed sexual relations with her ex-husband (as father substitute). She remembered her past in the seduction of her father. The loss of mother surrogates after her father's death ended her life for her, as these losses coincided with her emerging adolescent sexuality, which threatened repression and necessitated the regression to the more primitive defense of splitting. When she resumed her own sexual life, she hid it until I interpreted the maternal transference. She was unconscious of the need for a real relationship with me as a good, permissive mother. This, too, responded to interpretation.

What is most striking about this analysis is the long period during which, I, as the permissive, preoedipal mother, supported the emergence of cognitive functioning without which this patient could not have recalled and assimilated the incest trauma.

Mrs. L's analysis proceeded in a different way. I experienced her transference position as withholding, cold, and aloof and analyzed it in relation to her mother. She quickly identified with me and tried to hide the identification but it emerged in her anticipation of my competitive disapproval. When this transference distortion was analyzed, she began to recall closeness to her father accompanied by rage toward her mother. These feelings were expressed in the transference and in her creative writing. Analysis of the rageful nature of the maternal transference led to her ability to be involved emotionally with children and to contemplate pregnancy.

Her father's critical illness and rebuff of her attempts to reconcile with him recalled her parent's narcissistic use of her. She remembered an episode of sexual activity with a household workman and betrayal by a favorite aunt (mother symbol). This memory was later to be analyzed as a screen for and repetition of her earlier incest trauma. After that episode in latency, anal penetration became an obligatory masturbation fantasy, which she did not understand. When her wish to become pregnant was thwarted by her husband, she developed a regressive transference to me as the frustrating, unavailable mother and then a masculine identification with her father. Attempts to analyze this identification led to a list of physical complaints, which functioned as a resistance to analysis and later proved to represent a reenactment of the incest trauma. She had a dream revealing that a paternal transference was being resisted. Before this dream could be analyzed, a real event occurred in my life that made me sad in a way that only Mrs. L noticed. The transference then changed to one that revealed her caretaking responses to her depressed mother. She recalled sexual play with a little boy and became affectively aloof from me. Interpretation and working through of the maternal transference was followed by the hemorrhoid surgery. When I raised issues about her emotional reaction to the surgery, she developed warm feelings toward me. These were mutative in terms of her introjection of an involved maternal figure. *Again, the introjection of a caring, maternal figure is essential to the recovery of memories of the incest trauma.* Her next dream was pivotal, and her panic and my countertransference response to it enacted her need for a good maternal object. Thereafter, the history of the incest by forced anal rape was recovered. She also recovered an earlier memory of physical abuse by her mother and even has a pathological fracture that confirms this.

After the maternal abuse, she turned to her father for mothering as well as for gratification of her oedipal needs. These were reenacted with a boy neighbor, while her mother was depressed. The strengthening of her positive maternal identification through the analytic work and relationship then led to an interest in her mother's background and origins by way of her curiosity about my being Jewish. The consolidation of her positive identification with mother then allowed her to feel competitive with me. The maternal transference further progressed to an almost overwhelming negative transference, which required intensive analysis. Working through of these issues led to changes in her ego—she could let her defenses down, be a "declawed cat"; she could risk intimacy and a concurrent change in the transference to me. I was now seen as her good aunt.

In both of these patients, repair of the ego deficits seemed more dependent on the analysis of the consequences and conflicts related to maternal deprivation, than on uncovering the details of the incest experience itself. That the maternal relationship is more closely involved with the evolution of ego functioning should be of no surprise to experienced analysts. What needs emphasis, however, is the way in which the maternal deprivation can ensure and support the context in which incest may occur.

CONCLUSION

Patients with real rather than fantasied incest trauma may suffer severe damage in ego functioning. This damage includes a defective sense of ownership or control of the self, cognitive deficits with confusion and doubt of reality, defensive somatizations, identification with the aggressor, internally disturbed object representations (abusing parents), compromise in the ego's observing capacity, difficulty in establishing basic trust, the need for a real relationship with the analyst, vertical splitting, and compartmentalization of the incest trauma (which often extends to include peripheral events), depressive affect, and impairment of self-esteem. In addition, the recovery of memories of the incestuous events may only take place in the course of a long analysis and may be accompanied by intense feelings of panic and depersonalization.

The difficulty of conducting an analysis with a patient whose ego is significantly impaired is compounded by the potentially overwhelming countertransferences with which we may have to contend. These transferences may include our wish to aid our patients' denial, collude in their doubting, be drawn into a projective identification with their panic states, be frightened by the extent of their feelings of depersonalization. We must find a proper balance between the need to provide a reparative, caretaking relationship and the temptation to foresake the analytic stance for a supportive one.

While treating adults who were sexually abused as children is difficult at best, the situation is worse if we are not forewarned. It is therefore necessary that we be suspicious when we encounter the ego deformations described here. Only then can we be aware of potential transferences and countertransferences and enhance our ability to sustain the kind of thorough, complete, and lengthy analytic process that incest victims need in order to remember, work through, and repair the incest trauma, underlying deprivations, and resulting ego deficits.

REFERENCES

Bender, L. & Blau A. (1937), The reactions of children to sexual relations with adults. *Amer. J. Orthopsychiat.*, 7:500–518.

Blos, P. (1965), The initial stage of male adolescence. *The Psychoanalytic Study of the Child.*, 20:148–164. New York: International Universities Press.

Fliess, R. (1973), *Symbol, Dream and Psychosis*. New York: International Universities Press.

Freud, S. (1894), The neuropsychoses of defense. *Standard Edition*, 3:45–61. London: Hogarth Press, 1962.

_____ (1895), Studies on hysteria. *Standard Edition*, 2. London: Hogarth Press, 1955.

_____ (1896), The aetiology of hysteria. *Standard Edition*, 3:189–221. London: Hogarth Press, 1962.

_____ (1905), Three essays on the theory of sexuality. *Standard Edition*, 7:130–245. London: Hogarth Press, 1953.

_____ (1905), Fragment of an analysis of a case of hysteria. *Standard Edition*, 7:7–122. London: Hogarth Press, 1962.

_____ (1909), Notes upon a case of obsessional neurosis, *Standard Edition*, 10:155–318. London: Hogarth Press, 1955.

_____ (1916–1917), Introductory lectures on psychoanalysis. *Standard Edition* 15 & 16. London: Hogarth Press, 1963.

_____ (1931), Female sexuality. *Standard Edition*, 21:225–243. London:

Hogarth Press, 1961.

Freud, S. (1937), Moses and monotheism, *Standard Edition*, 23:1–137. London: Hogarth Press, 1964.

Ganzarain, R., Buchele, B. (1988). *Fugitives of Incest*. Madison, CT: International University Press.

Katan, A. (1973), Children who were raped. The *Psychoanalytic Study of the Child*, 28:208–225. New Haven, CT: Yale University Press.

Kestenberg, J. (1988), Psychological distress of holocaust survivors and offspring in Israel, forty years later: A review. *Israel J. Psychoanal.*, 24:244–256.

O'Brien, J. D. (1987), The effects of incest on female adolescent development, *J. Amer. Acad. Psychoanal.*, 15:83–92.

Margolis, M. (1977), A preliminary report of a case of consummated mother-son incest. The *Annual of Psychoanalysis*, 5:276–294. New York: International Universities Press.

Rascovsky, M. & Rascovsky, A. (1950), On consummated incest. *Internat J. Psycho-Anal.* 31:32–47.

Schimek, J. (1987), Fact and Fantasy in the seduction theory: A historical review. *J. Amer. Psychoanal. Assn.*, 35:937–965.

Shengold, L. (1963), The parent as sphinx. *J. Amer. Psychoanal. Assn.*, 11:725–751.

_____ (1974), The metaphor of the mirror. *J. Amer. Psychoanal. Assn.*, 22:97–115.

_____ (1979), Child abuse and deprivation: soul murder. *J. Amer. Psychoanal. Assn.*, 27:533–559.

_____ (1980), Some reflections on a case of mother-son incest. *Internat. J. Psycho-Anal.*, 61:461–475.

Wahl, C. (1960), The psychodynamics of consummated maternal incest. *Arch. Gen. Psychiat.*, 3:96–101.

6

Consequences of Childhood Sexual Abuse on the Development of Ego Structure
A Comparison of Child and Adult Cases

Susan P. Sherkow

In trying to assess the effect of sexual abuse in childhood on our adult patients, we have come full circle from where Freud began his theory of neurosis. We cannot assume accurate reporting by the patient who, in his history or in the course of treatment, claims to remember being sexually abused; nor can we assume that the patient has created a fantasy of abuse as a compromise between wish and defense. Furthermore, even if we had conclusive evidence that abuse had occurred, the complexity of material from an adult analysis makes it very difficult to pinpoint retrospectively the specific effect of sexual abuse on development. For one thing, sexual abuse by a family member seldom occurs as an isolated phenomenon, but rather usually occurs as part of an ongoing set of internal and external circumstances for the victim. Moreover, the role of the abuse on the intrapsychic mechanisms of the victim can hardly be teased apart from the multifaceted interaction with significant family members, both those involved and those who fail to be involved, that is, those who collude by denial or ignorance.

One means for gaining understanding of the specific consequences of sexual abuse on the ego development of our adult patients is to compare their cases with the case studies of children who are known to have been abused. Thus, our first task is to determine what effect, if any, sexual abuse has on the psychological development of the child and, if there is an effect, what the nature of it is.

Some authors addressing themselves to large populations of abused children and adults who were abused as children—Yorukoglu and Kemph (1966), Lukianowicz (1972), and Bender and Blau (1937)—have described cases of incest where they found no posttraumatic ill effects. A strong, positive relationship with the mother in the preoedipal period and solid ego defenses, including an ability to play "parent" to the errant parent, were seen as contributing to the ability of some of these children to weather the incestuous relationship. Westermeyer (1978) and Bender and Grugett (1952) have gone even further, describing brother-sister incest as nontraumatic when it provides love and attention to an otherwise emotionally deprived child; father-daughter incest, they feel, may serve the same purpose. These authors have also documented instances of single traumatic experiences of sexual abuse between a child and a nonfamily member, which, when handled thoughtfully and carefully by a loving family, left no documented sequelae.

Generally, however, most authors on this subject tell us that sexual abuse is bound to influence the intrapsychic development of the abused person, even if no sequelae are observable to the research eye. Long-term studies (see, for example, Kaufman, Peck, and Tagiuri, 1954; Steele and Pollack, 1968; Steele, 1970; Steele and Alexander, 1981; Steele, 1986) demonstrate such outcomes as prostitution or frigidity in women, homosexuality in men, and many instances of the development of neurosis, psychosis, and intergenerational repetitions of familial incestuous patterns. Moreover, case reports by the foregoing authors document how sexual abuse by a family member alters development by impairing the child's ability to develop parental trust, by interfering with oedipal development, by weakening the development of family ties, and ultimately by affecting the development of the sexual identity of the adult.

Clinically, the sexually abused child often presents with gross disturbances in behavior, such as sudden changes in appetite, sleep disturbance, temper tantrums, and exaggerated fears and anxiety. Symptoms in latency-age children also include a reluctance to attend school, fatigue, avoidance of usual activities and relationships, mood disturbances, and regressive oral behavior. Younger children may demonstrate avoidance of previously loved toys or people, bizarre behavior, sudden preoccupation with the genital difference and extreme interest in body parts, across-the-board regression vis à vis toilet training and use of bottle, or severe and prolonged outbursts of aggression both toward mother and other children.

Some children will openly acknowledge having been abused, but many deal with molestation by confession and retraction. The younger the child, especially under age two, the less likely the child will distinguish between fantasy and reality. Older children, out of guilt and a need to protect their parental ties, will often use massive denial and avoidance in order to ward off the memory of the abuse.

When evaluated in depth, older children may describe feeling exploited, worthless, and distrustful of any care, affection, or physical contact that they have been given. In very young children, obviously more totally dependent on the parent for control and limit setting, the destructive effect of abuse on the development of self-control and self-esteem may be very apparent in the child's play.

Elsewhere (Sherkow, 1990), I have suggested that it was possible to make a diagnosis of sexual abuse in a young child when one saw the following set of factors: intense sexualized play appearing very early in the course of consultation or treatment, with an emphasis on castration anxiety and fear of loss of object; a distinctive intensity and driven, compulsive quality of this play; preoccupation with one idiosyncratic kind of play to the exclusion of all others; the extremely hostile nature of regression in play, particularly in vicious attacks on dolls; stereotyping of symbolic play, especially phallic and thrusting play; exaggeration of normal curiosity about sexual issues and the genital difference; persistent confessions and retractions; and a preoccupation with fantasy versus reality—"Did I see it or did I make it up?"—sometimes expressed visually, as in "I saw it" or "I didn't see it."

From the psychoanalytic point of view, it seems necessary to analyze many abused children and adults in depth in order to gain a picture of the specific effect of sexual abuse on the many aspects of ego and character development. I would like, however, to make a start by presenting material from two case studies of children and then by comparing my observations of them with material from the case of an adult male.

CASE EXAMPLES: CHILDREN

Tina

Tina, whose diagnostic evaluation was more fully described elsewhere, was a two-and-3/4-year-old girl when she presented for evaluation of possible sexual abuse. She had told her brother during a bath that "Daddy put his fishies in my bottom and it hurt," pointing to her anus. She had been examining her genital area and playing "doctor," identifying Daddy as the doctor who played "fishies and butterflies" with her. After a summer holiday alone with her father, she developed a sleep disturbance, began to throw temper tantrums, claimed she "heard men walking in the middle of the night who were looking" at her while she was sleeping, showed poor appetite, and several times was found penetrating her vagina with objects.

Tina's play in the analysis demonstrated a preoccupation with dressing and undressing dolls, with making male dolls urinate, and with thrusting behavior that involved both the mouth, the vaginal area, and the anal area. Marked gender confusion was coupled with both the thrusting play and with references to urination and to the penis. The genital arousal that accompanied the play was discharged during the hour by frequent trips to the bathroom. It became clear that her play had the effect of exciting sexual "feelings" in her genital area as well as confusing her about the exact origin of the stimulation (vaginal, clitoral, or anal). Moreover, this behavior aroused hostile wishes toward her father and his penis, as well as anxiety about the potential loss of her father. These feelings resulted in a temporary symptom of masochistic, self-mutilating behavior, such as stabbing herself with a kitchen knife while trying to cut a cantaloupe on her knee. Further evidence of Tina's attempt to defend against her early oedipal wishes toward her father was found in her obsessively playing at cutting off pieces of dolls' bodies and then attempting to bandage them back on. She persistently bandaged and rebandaged the hurt limb. She showed an exaggerated interest in the genital difference, in urination, and in phallic-shaped objects. For instance, in her doll play she would spend hours trying to get the boy doll to "make pee-pee," calling him "her"; or in her game of "Monster" she would thrust the baby bottle into the boy doll's buttocks, called him "her," and then would give him the pink bottle to drink.

Tina's anger at her mother for failing to protect her heightened what would otherwise have been age-appropriate ambivalence toward her mother; it heightened, as well, her fear of abandonment by both parents, forcing further regression toward oral and anal self-comforting measures. Her behavior continued to suggest poor impulse control and self-destructiveness, impairment of reality testing, and poor body boundaries. The wish to be stimulated by her father, met by fear and guilt, kept alive an investment in impulses previously relinquished and also reinforced identification with the aggressor. The castration anxiety normally seen in a two- to three-year-old was exaggerated, and it ultimately seemed to interfere with the normative development of a female gender identity. Indeed, fears of separation from the object seemed to become fused with fears of loss of body parts and interfered with the development of identifications and hence with the organization of defenses, which otherwise might have helped her to cope with her guilt and shame. This consequently interfered with the development of her superego, as was manifest in the decrease of her impulse control. One would subsequently expect to see in a child like Tina either rigid superego development or the formation of superego lacunae.

Harriet

Another example of the role of sexual abuse in the distortion of ego and character development was seen in Harriet, who was referred for evaluation at the age of three and a half because her nursery school teacher had complained that Harriet had become severely withdrawn over a period of months. Previously a bright, cheerful, albeit quiet little girl, Harriet was now refusing to speak to or play with either the teacher or her classmates. In addition, Harriet had been withholding her stool, typically for between five and ten days at a time, necessitating the use of both purgatives and enemas, which were usually administered to her by her father. In her play at home, it was apparent to Harriet's parents that fantasy had come to replace reality; Harriet seemed to be living in a world of imaginary figures that she had created. Not only had Harriet withdrawn from her playmates, but she was irritable and extremely withholding from her mother. Once sweet-natured, she now often had temper tantrums and displayed enormous focused interest in her genitals, claiming that she "had a penis in there" (that is, in her vagina), and she masturbated openly and frequently.

Indeed, Harriet's relationship with her mother had deteriorated to the point where Harriet would not allow her mother to touch her or to show any expression of affection, not even a hug. This total physical rejection of her mother stood in stark contrast to Harriet's obvious infatuation with, and almost desperate clinging to, her father. Harriet also demanded to be in the bathroom with her father whenever he needed to bathe or urinate, although, according to Harriet's mother, he was oblivious to her coy interest in his penis.

Curiously, Harriet's parents mentioned—almost as an afterthought—Harriet's recent accusation that a teen-aged cousin, Joe, had put his penis in her mouth. When Joe and his mother had been confronted, both had denied Harriet's allegation. As Harriet's parents began to try to gather evidence to support or reject Harriet's claim, it appeared in retrospect more than likely that Joe indeed had been molesting Harriet periodically throughout the past year during his occasional visits to their home. As best as her parents could surmise, Joe had involved Harriet in touching and mouthing his penis; they did not know whether she had been penetrated, nor did they know whether he had played with her genitals.

Like Tina, Harriet began her first session by undressing all the dolls. She was preoccupied in her sessions with making the male dolls urinate and with forcing bottles and pacifiers into the boy dolls' mouths, using thrusting motions. Her facial expression and body tone during these sessions of focused play with dressing and undressing dolls, especially male dolls, showed intense preoccupation and body rigidity. She, like Tina, demonstrated marked genital confusion in trying to feed pink bottles to the male dolls or in putting pink diapers on male dolls and vice versa, as well as in trying to put female clothing on the male dolls. Her difficulty in differentiating fantasy from reality was evident in her play; for instance, in using water to play "pee-pee" with a doll, she became frantic that the "pee" had gotten on her clothes.

Harriet's ego development shows some of the same impairment that was seen in Tina. Her evident anger at her mother for not protecting her from the abusing situation nor, from the dynamic point of view, from her own oedipal wishes, heightened her ambivalence toward mother. As a result, Harriet developed the symptom of stool retention. The development of this symptom was further determined by the increased castration anxiety, which arose from her fear of the loss of her mother's love and approval because of Harriet's pleasure with the abusing situation, for example, her fascination with Joe's genitals. Regressive fears of separation were another factor embodied in the symptom. It is interesting that although the dynamics of Harriet's case were in many ways similar to those of Tina's, the choice of symptom—stool retention—stands in contrast to Tina's choice of symptom, which was anal explosive in nature. Both children, however, showed exaggerated interest in the voyeuristic and exhibitionistic aspects of genital-phase development.

DISTURBANCES OF EGO FUNCTION

The ego function that is primarily disturbed in sexually abused children appears to be reality testing. For these children, memories of real-life events related to the sexual abuse or abusing relationship are obscured, and fantasies "become" real. Many factors contribute to this phenomenon. As a response to the guilt over having participated in an activity that evokes fulfillment of a forbidden erotic wish, the child may identify with parental denial, obfuscation, or demands for secrecy in the use of repression, isolation, or denial of the sexual activity. The obverse of parental obfuscation also can be destructive: the "inno-cent" parent who insists on "talking about this and working it out," who dramatizes the discovery of incest, and who uses it against the child to punish the "abusing" parent (and, needless to say, the child, too) also creates a distortion in reality testing. The latter was the case with Tina, whose mother's tendency to overstimulate and "understand everything" heightened Tina's interest and anxiety about the incestuous experiences.

Another observable disturbance in ego function in sexually abused children is in the area of defense mechanisms. One notices a failure to establish adequate internal controls. Such disturbances in self-control will contribute to distortions of ego and superego that are stage specific. If a very young child is being abused, his bowel training, impulse control, and eating behaviors may be subject to marked disturbance. The younger the child, the more vulnerable she will be to disturbances in narcissism and to the predominant use of primitive defenses, such as projection, denial, use of action, and severe regression. Sadomasochistic trends seem to be strengthened or dominate development.

In older children masturbation may become inhibited or exaggerated. Intellectual aspects of ego functioning such as the ability to perceive, to conceptualize, and to learn from the environment may also be significantly affected.

In Harriet, we saw how the normal process of identification with parents, especially parental defense mechanisms, is inter-fered with. There is often an "as if" quality to these children's defensive systems. Harriet adopted pseudodefensive postures, mimicking each parent in turn. Father's style was obsessive, with major use of isolation, reaction formation, and denial; in his presence, Harriet appeared to avoid sexual material as well as any other affect-laden material and played at a highly sym-bolic level. Mother's style was anxious, depressed, but very expressive and confrontational; when with her, Harriet was more expressive and expansive and solicitous of her mother's mood and neediness. Similarly, because her mother hated dolls and never allowed Harriet to have any, it was some time before Harriet would allow herself to play with baby dolls in the play therapy in my office while mother was watching. (She confined herself to play with wooden figures, until her mother finally let her play with a doll outside of my office.)

Harriet also provides an example of how the demand for secrecy leads to withdrawal from and distrust of libidinal attachments. In sexually abused children, the role of voyeurism in development is enhanced or repressed excessively, and exhibitionism is often displaced onto body habitus, hair, and clothing. For example, during the period of her exposure to molestation, Harriet constantly refused to let her mother look at her, hold her, or pick out her wardrobe; she refused to wear anything her mother suggested or had touched.

Another factor commonly found is interference with symbolic functioning and sublimation; both Tina and Harriet used some toys in stereotypically symbolic fashion. For Tina, everything represented a phallus. In Harriet's case, her bowel movements represented "mommy," "baby," "mommy's lost baby," herself, her penis, and her sexual pleasure in play with her molester; yet initially she was unable to play with dolls in the usual way to represent self and object. As is typical, there was no neutralized ego available to allow her to enjoy playing for play's sake.

Another factor contributing to ego distortion is the chronic interference with object relations in these situations. The father, in part experienced as protector and comforter, is also the object of incestuous wishes. These must be split off from the perception of self as seductress and yet victim, whether or not father was the perpetrator. Any routine genital stimulation in nonsexual play with father is so reminiscent of the seduction and its exciting/ scary components that it must be avoided. In the case of actual incest with father, the split prevents integration of multiple aspects of the object relationship and may lead to the failure to integrate various positive and negative object images on all levels.

One particular resolution of these issues is demonstrated in the case of Harriet: she had to deny the seduction by Joe not only to protect the pleasurable aspect of the sex play, but also to protect oedipal fantasies, such as her enjoyment of taking father from mother. Therefore, she could not admit that Joe had hurt her, a denial that forced repression, regression, stool withholding, social isolation, and depression. Later, when treatment was significantly moving along, she related what can easily be seen as a beating fantasy: "Joe is bad. He hit me. We were in the kitchen. Daddy was making hot dogs, and Joe hit me. Daddy didn't see it—he didn't know it happened." Thus a beating fantasy emerges as repression of the sexual contact ensues, incorporating the elements of penis envy, voyeurism, confession, and retraction, perhaps ultimately making for a more positive resolution of her guilty participation in the seduction.

Additional implications for development of ego distortion, based on the study of Harriet and Tina, are that the sexual trauma intensifies the early castration anxiety of these little girls. This leads to loss of body boundaries; to across-the-board fear of loss of objects (before completion of separation-individuation, thus interfering with rapprochement); and to poor consolidation of self-esteem, perhaps irrevocably blurring the ability to discriminate self from object or to consolidate gender identity.

CASE EXAMPLE: ADULT

Mr. G

Mr. G was a 37-year-old, single writer when he came to me for a second analysis. He complained of anxiety, mixed phobias, and a renewed but repugnant preoccupation with homosexual fantasies. A previous analysis of 10 years' duration with a male analyst had helped him achieve his goal of renouncing active homosexuality, but he still found himself unable to form a heterosexual relationship despite his interest in women and his desire to get married.

Mr. G's father had been drafted into the army before the patient was born, and he did not know his father until he was three years old. During the intervening period, he and his mother lived with his maternal grandparents and his mother's younger brother and sister, who were both teenagers at the time. Mr. G adored his aunt and remembered having a very special relationship with her; he crawled into her bed for a "snuggle" on many occasions. He was still speaking to her almost nightly on the telephone.

Indeed, in his first analysis, his aunt had seemingly "stood in" for his mother whenever he dealt with erotic material that related to a maternal figure. He brought to his second analysis a portrayal of his mother that seemed to have remained intact (unanalyzed) from his youth, namely that she was a beautiful social butterfly concerned with appearances, preoccupied with her bridge games and fashion shows, and who used her son as a pawn in her relationship with her husband. Mr. G had few memories of her being "maternal" toward him or of her doing something that was specifically for his sake. What he did remember, however, was that she often paraded around the house half nude, was overly curious about his private conversations, monitoring his bedroom with an intercom, and was generally overly intrusive about his relationships in his teenage years with girls. Mr. G also perceived his mother as giving him "double messages" about his relationship to his father, such as encouraging him to battle with his father, but then insisting that he be the one to make up.

At the beginning of his reanalysis, the patient reported many "memories" involving his teenaged uncle, which appeared to be screen memories that had not been analyzed for their latent content in the previous analysis. These included "memories" of sleeping on the floor in his uncle's room, passing his uncle's room in the middle of the night and listening at the door, and seeing his uncle reading pornographic magazines.

The patient had had many symptoms in early childhood, including severe constipation over a long period of time. He had "memories" of being evacuated manually by his pediatrician, of being given enemas by one or more members of his grandparents' household, and of being fed purgatives. He was phobic of tea bags, of vomiting, and of the dark and "remembered" his grandfather trying to undo his fears by marching him around the dining room table dangling a tea bag in front of him. From his later childhood he remembered obsessive-compulsive rituals, including having to turn to look at his mother, who would be stationed at a particular dining room window when he left the house for school in the morning. His preoccupation with movies, especially musicals, and with record albums and certain movie stars amounted to a fixation; apparently the only thing that had distracted him from his fears was a promise to go to the movies, where he was usually taken by either his grandfather or his aunt.

Mr. G masturbated at least once a day from puberty until the present and reported having been preoccupied with his penis since early childhood. He was mortified that his penis was "crooked" and several times tried taping it to the side of his leg while he slept. He recalled letting his uncle's dog sniff at his penis, and when he was about 11 or 12 years old, he tried to get his aunt's daughter (aged three to four years) to touch his penis while they were bathing together. At about the age of 14, he began to engage in mutual masturbation with the "jocks" in his high school class and by age 18 was actively seeking homosexual encounters in public bathrooms. Nonetheless, he thought of himself as heterosexual and engaged in heavy petting with girls on whom he had crushes until he graduated from college.

At that point, his mother was diagnosed as having an incurable illness, and he flung himself into a period of driven homosexual activity, which he successfully hid from his family. He renounced such behavior during the course of his first analysis. Despite his overt homosexual behavior, his image of himself as a heterosexual persisted, and indeed, he was always in a state of profound but unrequited love with a woman.

Mr. G came into the treatment eager to please and to be the perfect patient. From the beginning of the analysis, we gradually understood that this behavior masked two important trends. First, he wanted to be such a "good boy" that I would never leave him or throw him out. A pattern emerged with his female employer wherein every time he felt threatened by her questioning his work, he would have a homosexual impulse to go to a pornographic movie theater and watch men engage in mutual masturbation. This phenomenon gradually took hold in the transference, and we began to see the same pattern of needing to act out a homosexual impulse following a fantasied rejection by me, such as a separation by a weekend or a holiday. Second, in wanting to be the perfect patient, he felt that it was his duty to report every thought, fantasy, action, and dream that had occurred since our prior meeting, as though that were "free association." It soon became apparent that he approached each hour as though it were a confessional. But despite his attempts to analyze himself, constantly making both transference and genetic interpretations for himself, both during and outside of the hours, he was obsessed with what was real and what was not. This self-doubting went beyond the question of whether he was "right" or "wrong." For example, having given me a lengthy interpretation of a sequence of events from the evening before, he would then become preoccupied with and anxious about whether his conclusions were the real truth or only an imagined truth. In the transference, he projected this phenomenon of "doubting" onto my remarks. Again, this questioning of my interpretation went beyond the issue of whether I was correct or not, as if he gave a double meaning to everything I said.

We also came to understand that Mr. G's need to contradict me in the service of "doubting" served the purpose of raising a barrier between us, as though his "Yes, but . . ." defined a boundary that prohibited a physical act occurring between us. We came to understand further that the nature of the physical act he most feared and wished for was to be masturbated by me.

At the same time, in analyzing the contents of the patient's reflections upon himself, I was struck that Mr. G persisted in seeing his aunt as the primary source of both maternal care and erotic stimulation, thereby excluding his mother from his self-analysis. As I began to question certain historical reconstructions about his aunt's role in his childhood, which he had made in his first analysis, it became apparent to me that his aunt must have been much less involved in his upbringing than he wished to believe and that he had succeeded in repressing or denying the years of daily care by his mother, especially after the age of three, when he and his parents lived 100 miles away from his grandparents, aunt, and uncle. For instance, although he had probably visited with his aunt on occasional weekends or holidays, she had married and moved to another state when he was six.

I began to explore with Mr. G the possibility that, as a way of denying the impact of anal and genital overstimulation, oedipal victory, but especially separation trauma and early castration anxiety, he had transferred onto his aunt nearly all the thoughts, wishes, and memories that belonged to his experience with his mother. He, in turn, began to report dreams and associations that related to his experiences at his grandparents' house.

We began to see that the "memories" he had preserved throughout his first analysis were screens for events that related to experiences with his uncle. Our understanding unfolded in the following way: associations to a dream about his uncle's dog sniffing at his penis led to his remembering presenting his erect penis to the dog and wondering, "What if she could talk and tell on me?" He remembered sleeping with the dog when he visited his grandfather's house, and although he knew the dog slept in his uncle's bedroom, he had not previously put together the probability that he had slept in the bedroom with his uncle on those visits. Gradually, he remembered that he had masturbated in front of the dog, again thinking to himself that the dog was asleep and that therefore she was not going to pay much attention to him. He wondered about why he thought he had been responsible for the dog's death and if that had anything to do with his guilt about whether something sexual had transpired between himself and his uncle. This musing was followed by a dream in which "things are not what they seem." In the dream his uncle appeared wearing a cashmere robe that turned into a smoking jacket with three loops in back (instead of the two belt loops one would expect to find). These "three loops" represented the phallic triad. In ensuing sessions, memories emerged of needing to watch his uncle masturbate, feeling glued to the spot, fascinated, not being able to leave the scene even though he felt threatened and felt a sense of danger. The transference manifestation of this behavior was apparent in the increasingly sexual nature of the "confessional" aspect of the patient's associations. He would be alarmed at my silence, feeling that he was not doing a good enough job in keeping me interested, which meant that he should either change the subject to keep my attention or recount homosexual wishes or memories of past experiences to "keep the analyst at the door." Both the exhibitionistic aspect—keeping his mother at the door watching him— and the voyeuristic aspect—feeling glued to the door himself, watching mother—were apparent.

Gradually the associations to watching his uncle masturbate were connected with the old fears of vomiting, which for a time recurred as a transient symptom in the treatment. Mr. G would lie awake all night, afraid of throwing up. We were then able to connect his fear of the teabag with his fear of the dark and of throwing up; possibly he had been molested in the dark by something that connected to the feeling or visual experience of a teabag. "Perhaps," he said, "a wet teabag felt like pubic hair or like squeezing a flaccid penis." He became convinced that his fear of vomiting was a fear (or wish) for fellatio, and we were able to interpret that the symptom of being afraid of vomiting represented being trapped with the wish to put the penis in his mouth while watching his uncle masturbate but being afraid of gagging on it. "I don't know if I gagged because I *did* put the penis in my mouth or only wished to. *I don't know*—I guess it doesn't matter." He then remembered that at age 17 he stayed with his eight-year-old male cousin and rubbed his penis against his cousin's arm while his cousin was sleeping. *The cousin did not know it was happening.*

Soon after, he had a dream in which he was showing something sexual to a man who was masculine but effete. "He and I both have erections. He masturbates both of us simultaneously." The man reminded him of various movie stars, all of whom looked like his uncle.

Mr. G then dreamed that he was being chased from a tranquil place into a subway station by a man who wanted to rape him by giving him a "blow job." He was distracted by the presence of a little boy who was standing there, watching. In the dream, the patient cried, "No! A little kid is here and he'll be traumatized if he sees it." Someone said, "Don't be ridiculous! He [the little boy] is 17 years old and has been out on a date." The next part of the dream occurred after oral sex had taken place. Mr. G was ashamed and felt terribly guilty. Suddenly he saw an actress whom he had often identified with his mother, as if she had been the one who had been raped. "I was upset not for me but for her, and then she said, 'Don't worry, I wanted it to happen.'"

In his associations, he again remembered coming home from a date at age 17, going into the bedroom he was sharing with his eight-year-old cousin, being *tempted* to rub his penis on his cousin's arm and thinking, "This is ridiculous—a dangerous and foolish thing to do. What if he were to wake up and see me standing here? I got back into bed and went to sleep." At this point, Mr. G had repressed his earlier confession with regard to the same incident. He remained convinced, however, that his uncle must have been about 17 when his uncle performed fellatio on him or engaged the patient in mutual fellatio. Three weeks later, Mr. G had another dream: "I had a puppet in my hand and I grabbed its crotch in a pinching fashion, like I was rubbing out an insect with my thumb. Then I had the thought, 'That's proof that I was molested as a child,' just like children who testify in court using dolls to illustrate what happened to them."

Further dreams and associations exposed evidence of sexualized behavior with his mother and possibly his grandfather as well. Once he began to acknowledge the very real role mother had played in his upbringing, he remembered, for example, that she "stripped to the waist at the basin [in his presence] in order to wash her underarms while getting dressed to go out to dinner." Another memory that emerged was of standing guard near his parents' bedroom door every Sunday night in order to hear them having intercourse, hearing his mother protest loudly, and "wondering why she went back in there every Sunday night." He eventually came to wonder whether his grandfather behaved in some masturbatory or homoerotic way toward him when the grandfather took him to the movies during his youth. He even speculated whether grandfather had not been the source of the sexual disturbance in the family, possibly having molested all three of his children to one extent or another, which would explain to Mr. G why all three had such severe narcissistic difficulties.

DISCUSSION

Like the molested children described earlier, Mr. G demonstrates a typical preoccupation with the question, "Did it happen, or did I make it up?" Over his lifetime, Mr. G had created for himself a series of constructions, that is, fantasies, which he took to be real, and which were so convincing that a previous, 10-year analysis had left them intact. By the same token, he had obscured real-life events and convinced himself and his analyst that what was real was "only fantasy." Typically, he would say about a memory, "I can't remember it; I'm making this up as if it really happened."

The demands for secrecy in hiding his uncle's molestation of him, and later his mother's exhibitionism, had a marked effect on the development of his identity. We began to understand how the excitement of participating in sexual behavior with his uncle made him so profoundly guilty that he could not confide in, or enjoy warmth or tenderness from, his father. Like Harriet and Tina, Mr. G could not enjoy being cared for by his mother, whose failure to protect him both made him enraged at her and exaggerated his wishful fantasies to seduce her, just as he saw himself seducing his uncle. The guilty perception of himself as seductor was compounded by the seductive behavior of his aunt, who, although she apparently did not engage in overt sexual behavior with him as a young boy, reinforced his erotic fantasies toward her and made herself ultimately the benefactor of all such wishes that originated in his feelings toward his mother.

Moreover, the "double-talk" by his mother, in which she seduced the patient by getting him to fight with his father over demands that father refused but that mother ultimately met, was seen to be another form of the mother's exhibitionism, which perpetuated the confusion between what was fantasy and what was real. This confusion interfered with Mr. G's development at every stage; impeded his control over infantile impulses to smear, to be violent, to gorge, or to starve; and prevented him from learning such control by identification with either parent, or anyone else for that matter, just as we saw in the cases of Harriet and Tina.

In the course of Mr. G's analysis, we reconstructed that he had developed the symptom of stool retention during early childhood in response to being molested, as was the case with Harriet. He frequently experienced a need to "eat sweets" in response to homosexual impulses. His preoccupation with his body was out of proportion to the overall high level of his general ego functioning. Like Harriet's, his voyeuristic and exhibitionistic impulses were displaced onto his clothes and hair. For example, in the past, after he had had a homosexual encounter, he was never again able to wear the clothing that he had worn during the encounter without being reminded of the incident. If he felt guilty enough about the encounter, he would throw the clothing away.

As we saw in the case of Harriet, Mr. G's defensive structure had an "as if" quality to it. In his thinking, he appeared to be obsessive, but his behavior overall was not in keeping with a diagnosis of an obsessive-compulsive disorder. A brilliant man whose successful career depended on his ability to think, reason, and write creatively, he had a highly organized faculty for symbolic functioning on the intellectual and verbal levels. This capacity, however, did not serve a positive defensive purpose in protecting him from his impulses or from the anxiety they generated, just as with Harriet and Tina. They also demonstrated highly symbolic functioning, for example, in their play, which was an exaggerated extension of their sexual trauma but similarly did not defend successfully against the conflict and anxiety elicited by the trauma. In fact, Mr. G, despite his seemingly high level of organization and appropriate social behavior, used the primitive defenses of projection, physical avoidance, denial, and action instead of words. He evinced diminished reality testing of the kind one expects to see with such primitive defenses and a substitution of "is it real or is it just my imagination" as a defense against raw impulses. "Do I *really* want to do this, or do I just *think* I want to do this?" permeated his thinking, as a substitute for any kind of sexual activity, whether heterosexual or homosexual in nature. This phenomenon began to be clarified as a response to his wish/fear of being invaded sexually by a powerful man in the transference insofar as the analyst represented his powerful father. Gradually, then, the underlying sadomasochistic trends were elucidated. Mr. G could begin to talk in the sessions about the sadistic homosexual fantasies he imagined during masturbation, and for the first time he became aware of a fleeting heterosexual thought in the few seconds prior to ejaculation.

The typical preoccupation of the adult who has been molested in childhood with the question "Did it happen, or did I make it up?" also poses technical problems for the analyst. From the pragmatic point of view, the analyst might feel it is important to help the patient distinguish between what actually happened in childhood and what was wished for. Reconstruction becomes especially difficult where overdetermination includes the element of establishing what was likely versus what was true. Furthermore, reconstruction is made difficult by virtue of the patient's need to repress the guilt-laden memories of sexually traumatic events, and their role in shaping the ego development of the adult is thus equally difficult to tease apart from all of the concomitant factors in the patient's development.

The following sessions illustrate some of the complications the analyst confronts in trying to assess the effect of explicit molestation on the reconstruction of incestuous wishes and developmental issues as they appear in the transference.

In one session, Mr. G reported a dream about W (his current, unrequited love): "W is watching me try to make love to another woman. I am unable to maintain my erection and eventually the woman I am making love to turns into W." In his associations to the dream he confessed to feeling terribly guilty about coming late to that hour. He then remembered feeling afraid of being trapped in a car the day before on the way to his session. What if he needed to have a bowel movement? I interpreted to him that he was afraid of being trapped in my office for fear of having an erection that he could not control and that should I see it, I might find him inadequate.

At the beginning of the next hour, Mr. G announced that he needed to change one of his session times during the following week because of what he thought was an unavoidable conflict with his work. He wanted to know whether he could have a make-up hour. When I did not answer, he said that he didn't understand my rules. Why didn't I answer? He then began to doubt that he really needed to cancel the hour. He declared that W was on his mind; he was angry at her. He wondered whether she had been manipulating him, using him to get a part in his next production. He bemoaned how she taunted him. He then remembered a dream about feeling claustrophobic on an airplane. He was nauseated and felt panicky about being trapped. I interpreted this memory of his dream as a response to feeling hurt and humiliated not only by W, whom he suspected of using him, but by me, whom he suspected of using him for his money when I refused to give him a change of hour.

Suddenly, he remembered that he had forgotten to bring a check. He commented again on my silence on the subject of the change in the hour and then reported feeling sick, as if he had the flu. "I feel trapped when you don't answer my question." I said, "You don't know what I'm thinking." His immediate association was: "I don't know why, but it makes me think of incest, of that time when I exposed myself in the bath to F [a cousin]. I was ten and she was three. My grandfather was in the bathroom, too. I wonder if the reason my grandmother had no sense of humor was because she knew about all the incest going on around her. I remember my grandfather saying it wasn't nice for me to be undressed in front of my cousin, but I still felt he was titillated. Was I really in the tub with her or just there urinating?" He was immediately reminded of an incident that had happened on an airplane. A woman was showing off her child in a way that reminded him of his mother taking him to a tea room as if he were her "little date." He hated her for it and felt used by her instead of loved. He remembered how she had been so proud at having gotten her son, "the little gentleman," to help her with her coat in the tea room.

Again, he referred to W, with all "her fucking money" and the irony that he was being used by her when all the while he felt he had been the one to be taking advantage of her because he was so in love with her. "You should have seen through her and stopped me." I responded by pointing out that he needed to know what I was thinking at all times because he must have been afraid that when I was silent I was harboring incestuous thoughts toward him, just as he had been afraid his mother was seducing him when she pitted him against his father. In his associations he remembered how much he wished his father were dead, how much he wanted his mother for himself. "I hated my father. I wanted him to go away. I remember consciously wishing he would leave, or be dead, or at the very least divorce my mother. In college, I had conscious fantasies of sneaking home and murdering him in bed and then sneaking back to college. It would be a perfect alibi. My mother and I would be free to enjoy life together. I loved our trips alone together to [a big city]." I remarked that it looked as if his angry ideas about her seducing him were a reaction to his feeling hurt and rejected, that, although mother loved him and behaved seductively toward him, she never left his father. He then wondered *where to draw the line*—Did she lead him on more than a mother normally does? Was she, indeed, more incestuous with him? Or was it his wishful imagination, for example, when she took him to the tea room as on a date rather than letting him play outside with other kids?

A year later, Mr. G reported a dream: "I am watching two parents with their baby girl. On second thought, I'm not sure the father is there. The mother is helping extract stool while the baby is defecating. It's not too disgusting because the bowel movement is coming out on its own. The baby is in a bathinet. I know that sounds like a slip, but that was the word I dreamed. Then the baby turns over and is urinating from his penis and I am surprised; I didn't expect the baby to be a boy, and his penis is bigger than I expected, as if it was erect." In his associations he thought about our understanding that he treated his work as though he had to display a perfect product, as in toilet training. He remembered recent homosexual fantasies, being repulsed by the thought of urinating on someone, but being aroused if someone watched him urinate.

He then remembered another dream: "My grandmother was encouraging me to have incest with somebody, but no one was there. It was vague as to who it was. There's an image of a bed with sheets but no one in it. I was worried that my mother would see, but my grandmother said, 'Don't worry, she's asleep.' I know that she meant that metaphorically, that my mother was impervious, unaware, wouldn't bother to notice or was incapable of noticing." He then pointed out that it was ironic that he had had this dream because his grandmother was the only one he did not suspect of being involved in incest in the family.

He wondered if these dreams were inspired by the fact that his uncle was in town and that he had had dinner with him the night before. In his associations he referred to his toilet training, and it emerged that he was "ignorant" of whether or not his own penis became erect, or whether he felt any sensation in his penis during urination. He also admitted, in associating to the position of the baby's penis in the dream, that he did not know whether babies had an erection during urination, that is, that he did not "know" about the anatomical function of the penis. He suddenly recollected a rhyme that would occur to him during urination, especially if he had to urinate badly: "Pissorama gramma." He then recalled that his grandmother had taught him how to urinate standing up, by holding on to his penis; but the memory stemmed from a time when he must have been more than four years old, which he thought was too old to be first learning how to urinate standing up.

By pretending not to know, or acting as if he were ignorant (as he said his mother was in the dream), or being "asleep" to incest, (to his erotic interest in the activity), he could get his grandmother to hold his penis while he urinated; and in the transference he could get me to talk about it as if I were holding his penis. More specifically, he tried to induce me to "educate" him about his penis and how it functioned when he urinated as a verbal displacement from the wish to have me actually hold his penis and "educate" him manually the way he remembered his grandmother doing. Whether or not he "remembered" his grandmother educating him as a screen for the more forbidding event of his mother educating him is open to question. In either case, the resultant characteristic of "pseudoimbecility" about the functioning of his own body allowed him to perpetuate gratification of the erotic wish without having to suffer the consequences of rejection were he to "know" how to use his penis in intercourse with a woman.

SUMMARY

In comparing the two child patients and the adult patient, we find that the implications for development of ego disturbances that were seen in the children were seen as well in the adult, namely, intensification of early castration anxiety, body-boundary disturbance, fear of object loss, interference with rapprochement, interference in consolidation of self-esteem, blurring of the ability to discriminate between self and object, and interference with consolidation of gender identity. In addition, certain features of the play behavior seen in the children were exaggerated in the adult patient, such as stereotyping of symbolic functioning and anomalous use of primitive defenses such as massive denial, avoidance and loss of impulse control in the context of an otherwise relatively intact and highly developed ego organization. Finally, the preoccupation with the question of fantasy versus reality was pronounced in both the child and the adult cases.

The relative consistency of some themes in the cases of Tina, Harriet, and Mr. G will, it is hoped, be the basis for further study of cases of molested children and adults.

REFERENCES

Bender, L. & Blau, A. (1937), The reaction of children to sexual relations with adults. *Amer. J. Orthopsychiat.*, 7:500–518.

_____ Grugett, A. E., Jr. (1952), A follow-up report on children who had atypical sexual experience. *Amer. J. Orthopsychiat.*, 22:825–827.

Kaufman, I., Peck, A. L. & Tagiuri, C. K. (1954), The family constellation and overt incestuous relations between father and daughter. *Amer. J. Orthopsychiat.*, 24:266–279.

Lukianowicz, N. (1972), Incest: Paternal incest. *Brit. J. Psychiat.*, 120:301–313.

Sherkow, S. P. (1990), The evaluation and diagnosis of sexual abuse in little girls. *J. Amer. Psychoanal. Assn.*, 38:305–327.

Steele, B. F. (1970), Parental abuse of infants and small children. In: *Parenthood*, ed. E. Anthony & T. Benedek. Boston: Little, Brown, pp. 449–477.

_____ (1986), Some sequelae of sexual maltreatment of children. Unpublished manuscript.

_____ Alexander, H. (1981), Long-term effects of sexual abuse in childhood. In: *Sexually Abused Children and Their Families*, ed. P. B. Mrazek & C. H. Kempe. Oxford: Pergamon Press, pp. 223–233.

_____ Pollack, C. B. (1968), A psychiatric study of parents who abuse infants and small children. In: *The Battered Child*, ed. R. E. Helfer & C. H. Kempe. Chicago: University of Chicago, pp. 103–147.

Westermeyer, J. (1978), Incest in psychiatric practice: A description of patients and incestuous relationships. *J. Clin. Psychiat.*, 39:643–648.

Yorukoglu, A. & Kemph, J. P. (1966), Children not severely damaged by incest with a parent. *J. Amer. Acad. Child Psychiat.*, 51:111–124.

7

Incest as Trauma
A Psychoanalytic Case

Judith N. Huizenga

Nancy, a 35-year-old analytic patient who first had sexual intercourse with her father at the age of nine, dreamed that she hemorrhaged from her vagina and called out to me for some protective pads. In her dream, I replied that she could handle this on her own, and, dripping blood, she left my office, desperate but knowing that her bleeding was not fatal. During the analytic hour that followed, Nancy associated to the fantasy of being ripped up by a knife in her uterus and wondered if she had bled after intercourse with father. She spoke of feeling that her mother had not heard her distress or recognized her need for help. I commented on her fear that I could not help her with this injury, this feeling of having a ripped-out uterus. She replied, "Life is a search. A good therapist makes use of the present, but does not forget the past. But will you be able to make up for the past?"

Nancy's dream occurred 12 months into a 40-month analysis. It revealed her unconscious fantasy of the damage caused by the incest—her father had ripped her genitals and uterus. Prior to the dream, Nancy had felt inadequate as a woman and mother and believed that her genitals were different from those of other women. She was unaware that the roots of these feelings were connected, in part, to her experience of the incest. Subsequent to the dream and its analysis, the consequences of the incest became affectively engaged for this patient in a very meaningful way.

Dreams such as Nancy's dramatically illustrate the enduring psychological damage caused by incest. Through psychoanalysis, we can understand the intrapsychic impact of this trauma and find a way to repair the incest wound. Before Nancy and I could arrive at a point at which we might successfully analyze her dreams, however, I had to help her strengthen certain psychological capacities—notably those of symbolization and fantasy formation—so that her dreams could be more meaningfully connected to the conflicts that they attempted to represent. In the material that follows, I present a summary of Nancy's analysis, with a particular focus on her dreams, to illustrate the traumatic effects of incest and its impact on Nancy's capacities for symbolization and fantasy formation. First, however, I would like to say a few words about psychological trauma, dreams, symbolic capacity, and fantasy.

Laplanche and Pontalis (1973, p. 456) and Dowling (1987) each use the term "psychological trauma" to refer to an external event in a patient's life that is defined by its intensity, by the patient's inability to respond to it adequately in a psychological sense, and by the upheaval and long-lasting effect that it brings about in the psychical organization. Their views build on those of Freud (1926), who understood trauma as an experience of the helplessness on the part of the ego, and Krystal (1978), who emphasized the significant effect that childhood trauma has on symbolization, fantasy formation, and the capacity to verbalize emotion.

Father–daughter incest produces an intrapsychic trauma that can reverberate throughout the child's life. The external event of the incest and its effect on future relationships and the patient's adult sexuality have been well described (see Herman, 1981, for a summary of the general psychiatric literature). For my patient, Nancy, the experience of the incest became grafted onto an already existing oedipal fantasy that had been reinforced by a traumatic separation from her mother when Nancy was 5 years old. It was this amalgamation of fantasy and reality that gave rise to many intense, conflicting feelings.

Dowling (1987, p. 50) described dreams as a window opening

into a patient's response to trauma, a window that would otherwise have been closed. De Saussiere (1982, p. 168) noted that in posttraumatic states, dreams may express fantasies that were part of the original traumatic situation or that were developed in response to the trauma. He also described how the trauma itself may distort the symbolic capacity of the dreamer's ego, thereby blocking the effective use of symbols to represent elements of the trauma, the conflicts that the trauma gave rise to, and their associated connections with other elements of the dreamer's psyche. This situation is analogous to that of the disruption of play in children when anxiety overwhelms their symbolic capacities. Thus, DeSaussiere reported that dreams dealing with the residues of early childhood trauma often seem nightmarish, frightening, and real. These dreams are in contrast to nonposttraumatic state dreams, which can be satisfying and can lead to a reduction of psychic tension and physical relaxation (p. 168).

These considerations are particularly relevant to the case of Nancy, whose incest experience began during latency. As Sarnoff (1976) reminds us, symbolization and fantasy are two of the major mechanisms by which the latency-age child defends against and integrates sexual and aggressive drives and conflicts. Thus, one would not be surprised to find severe constriction in Nancy's capacities to dream, play, fantasize, and symbolize, which indeed was the case.

Prior to analysis and in its early stages, Nancy's dreams connected to the incest were repetitive and anxiety producing and seemed "real" to her. She awoke from them in fear in the middle of the night and could be comforted only by lying in her husband's arms. She had few associations to these dreams, other than their reminding her of the fact of the incest itself. In the course of the analysis, and as a result of the conflicts that were worked through, Nancy's dreams changed, becoming richer in symbols, fantasies, and associations. In both latent and manifest content, they reflected the familiar themes of the incest: the seduction, the absence of her mother's protection, her identification with the aggressor, and the perception of being a damaged victim. Her perception of protection by the analyst/mother, her identification with the analyst as a strong woman, and the recovery of positive memories of both parents that predated the incest reflected components of her successful working through of the trauma.

Like so many other victims of parent–child sexual abuse, Nancy suffered a double betrayal in the incestuous act. First was the experience of overwhelming sexual stimulation and the breaking of boundaries between fantasy and reality by the father. Second was the simultaneous lack of protection by the mother. As much as a little girl might desire her father, she must be allowed to feel secure that sexual contact between them will not occur. Without this sense of assurance, a child cannot feel free to play with symbols and fantasies. Thus, after an incestuous act, no matter how much it may correspond to a little girl's secret or unconscious desires, she is likely to feel used and abused by her father. She may experience unbearable conflicts about her sexual and aggressive feelings, especially those feelings aroused in relation to the incest, and her sense of the boundary between reality and fantasy may be weakened. Often, incest victims remain silent about their experiences, thereby cutting themselves off from help from their mothers and other adults. The secrecy deprives them of mothering, comfort, and protection.

In adulthood, relationships with husband and children may also suffer from this betrayal. Nancy could not trust herself or those she loved. She feared sexual intimacy with her husband because her sexual feelings brought back memories of the incest. She avoided closeness with her children because she feared that she would fail to protect them from her own sexual desires. The incest experience dominated Nancy's image of herself. She felt damaged, like a victim. She identified with her father's aggressiveness in order to protect herself from feelings of being powerless, feelings that contributed in turn to a confusion about her identity as a woman.

Nancy first consulted me several years after a previous, moderately successful course of psychotherapy. She was seeking further treatment for panic attacks, obsessional thoughts, and sexual inhibitions. In our intitial consultations, she mentioned the incest but did not seem to appreciate the enormous impact that it had had on her development. We began with twice-weekly sessions during which she reported incest-related dreams that were realistic, repetitive, and anxiety provoking. Her only associations were to the incest act. These terrifying realistic dreams connected to the trauma showed that the mechanisms of displacement, symbolization, and repression had failed to defend her against the conflicts and fear produced by the trauma. It was exactly this problem that made me consider analysis for Nancy. I hoped that through the work and protection of the analysis, she could enhance her capacities to use symbols and metaphors in her dreams and fantasies, restore blocked connections between her present life and past events, enrich her associational stream, and liberate her affects, all in the service of helping her to reconstruct the events and meaning of the incest and work through the intrapsychic damage it had produced.

Actually, Nancy had suffered two major traumas in her childhood. When she was five years old, her mother abandoned the family in an attempt to escape from the continual fights caused by Nancy's father's temper and demands. She told Nancy that she was going shopping and did not return for six months. Although Nancy and her two younger sisters were left in the adequate care of her father and grandmothers, she felt responsible for her mother's abandoning her and feared she would never see mother again. She blamed herself for the abandonment, believing that her mother had left her because she was too much like her father—demanding, stubborn, disobedient, and often angry. She recalled squirming when her parents tried to hold her and having to be chased by her father in the airport. When Nancy was a toddler, her mother had tied her to a table, and she had dragged the table off the porch to play in the street. We later came to see how her abandonment had reinforced Nancy's oedipal longings for her father, paved the way for the incest by reinforcing her tendency to turn to him, rather than her mother, for emotional comfort, and probably reinforced the father's tendency to seek comfort from Nancy rather than from his wife.

In addition, Nancy had particularly resented the birth of her sister, 18 months younger. After her sister was born, she recalled, she had put her doll in the street and watched a truck run it over. Later, after mother had left her, Nancy worried that she would accidentally hurt her sisters, whom she described as "whiney" and "cry babies." Upon her mother's return, Nancy's behavior changed abruptly into that of a responsible, obedient, and helpful child. She felt that she had to look after her mother, whom she now described as a martyr, resigned to the tyranny of her husband. Subsequently, her father became increasingly angry and tyrannical as the financial situation of the family worsened.

The second trauma, for which the first trauma may have been an important predisposing factor, was the incest. This trauma occurred from Nancy's 9th to 11th year, during which time her father had sexual intercourse with her on about eight occasions. He would approach her from the back. She had no memory of his touching her. She recalled his asking if he was hurting her, that she replied no, and that afterwards, he wiped his penis with a handkerchief. During the sex act, Nancy felt frightened, numb, "as if I was not there." Her father stopped approaching her for sex only after her repeated refusals. Before the incest, she had adored her father; later in the treatment Nancy would recall many happy times with him, swinging in the hammock and swimming in the nearby lakes. She had felt special with her father and compatible in spirit. After the incest, she detested him and felt guilty. She avoided him and stayed close to her mother. She told no one of the incest until she was an adult.

Despite her terrible secret, Nancy functioned extremely well away from home. She was a popular and excellent student who enjoyed both girl friends and boy friends. She moved away for college and graduate school, obtained a master's degree in occupational therapy, and married a kind man whom she loved but to whom she was not sexually attracted. She did not experience symptoms until after her marriage. Following a visit to her parents' home, she had her first panic attacks and nightmares. She confessed to her husband that she felt sexually frigid and shared with him her memories of the incest. She subsequently entered psychotherapy for several years with a male therapist with good results. Her panic attacks decreased and her fear of separation diminished; she was more responsive sexually and became orgasmic with masturbation. Although she became able to enjoy the intimacy of the sexual act, she remained inorgasmic during intercourse.

During the next decade, Nancy functioned as a well-integrated obsessional character. She succeeded at work and enjoyed her marriage. However, conflicts over her unconscious dependency on her husband, as well as residues of the incest, interfered with her finding her husband sexually exciting. She enjoyed her pregnancy and motherhood. On the surface, she appeared to be an excellent mother who listened carefully to her son and helped him with his school work. She remained somewhat distant from him, however, to avoid angry or sexual feelings. Her son responded to her distance by having tantrums, which seemed designed to increase his closeness to his mother. Nancy had no close relationships with other women with whom to share concerns or seek advice. She was distant and critical of her female colleagues, who, she felt, were victims, like her mother.

It was the persistence of these symptoms and character problems that led Nancy to consult me about returning to psychotherapy. Initially, she felt that I, a woman therapist, could not help her because I would be ineffective, like her mother. During the opening phase, a twice-weekly psychotherapy that lasted for several months, she forgot the material from session to session and forgot about me during absences. Although she recalled the facts of the incest and the earlier abandonment, she recounted these events with no apparent affect. As mentioned earlier, she had repeated nightmares. In one, she was being chased by a naked man. In another, her father was in bed with her. She was unable to use these dreams to further her therapy or to work productively with them. After six months, I felt, and explained to Nancy, that we were unable to marshall sufficient therapeutic intensity and focus to affect her symptoms in a twice-weekly psychotherapy and recommended psychoanalysis. Nancy accepted reluctantly. Gradually, the increase in frequency to four times a week. and the psychoanalytic setting, proved extremely helpful. The therapeutic alliance and positive transference provided sufficient support and protection to allow Nancy to experience the painful memories and conflicts about her past evoked by the transference, dreams, and associations.

At first, Nancy distanced herself from the analytic material by speaking in a superficial and detailed manner. If she allowed herself to associate freely, she would stop herself, saying that she felt as though her father were coming in the room. She also had to protect herself against recognizing her anger toward her sisters. This defensive stance was expressed in a dream in which she observed her neighbors over the backyard fence but pretended not to notice what was happening. In reality, the neighbor's father had committed suicide, but he was represented as alive in the dream. Her own father, although still alive, had died as a parent for her after the incest. This "over the fence" distance and pretending not to notice represented major defenses against her recognition of the incest. Within a few months of starting the analysis, however, Nancy was associating more freely and expressing feeling of fear, anger, and sadness. She no longer watched herself and others from "over a fence."

By the sixth month of analysis, Nancy acknowledged my help with her overwhelming feelings when she dreamed we built a dam together to prevent a flood and then dreamed that we removed a road block, which she connected with her newly gained access to her feelings about the past and the present. Once she began to let herself see and acknowledge what she felt, we learned that Nancy initially had felt seduced into analysis, unable to refuse my offer of closeness, as she had been unable to refuse the sexual advances of her father. As her feelings of being seduced into the analysis were clarified, she had dozens of dreams of seduction, dreams filled with the naked bodies of men and women. For example, in relation to her feelings of being forced to have an analysis, she dreamed of being tightly held by a naked woman with a penis and of squirming in the woman's arms. She associated to her fear of being overwhelmed by her feelings toward her father that were emerging as a result of the psychoanalytic process. She was aware of her sexual excitement toward me in the paternal transference and felt that our laughter together was erotic, seductive. The awareness of her feelings of being seduced by me into her analysis stimulated her desire to say "No!" to me—the "No!" that had taken almost three years for her to say to father when she was a child. She then enacted her refusal to be seduced by canceling or requesting changes in our appointments. She also pushed me away by criticizing me, as she did her husband. The strengthened therapeutic alliance and her excellent observational skills allowed her to note the origin of these feelings.

In contrast to what had transpired in psychotherapy, Nancy now experienced separations as abandonments. She worried that I would leave her as her mother had if she had too much energy or if she was too stubborn or angry. She also worried that she might hurt her son, as she had worried about hurting her sisters when her mother left. These fears were particularly pronounced during weekends and other times when we did not meet. In response to the impulses that underlay these fears, she developed a compulsion of putting knives out of sight and worried that her son might be harmed or molested by a stranger.

When I left for a vacation, it stirred memories of her mother's departure. "Vacation" became "termination." On my return, Nancy poignantly described her feelings of abandonment and calling out, sobbing, for her mother. She recalled her fears at night during her mother's absence and worried that I, like her mother, would leave her because I could not stand her energy and anger. She remembered being a good, compliant daughter with no sad or angry feelings after her mother's return.

Later, after a year of analysis and faced with an upcoming separation, she dreamed that I left her and that her former therapist reassured her that I would return. She reported that she had shut down her feelings over the weekend so as not to miss me and not to be left alone with feelings that were too difficult for her. Once more, when left with her angry feelings—this time at me—she feared hurting her son, as she had feared hurting her sisters when she was five.

In the course of our work, Nancy became aware that after the incest her father had died for her as a parent. In a dream, her father had to be shot to stop him from attacking her with a knife. I interpreted this as her wish for revenge toward her father, because of the harm he had done her. She replied that she hated him and wanted to tell him of her suffering and inability to have sexual feelings. Her anguish, so poignantly expressed in her analytic hours, seemed undiminished by the decades.

In a dream of Euripides' tragic character Medea cradling her dead children in her arms, Nancy expressed the failure of her parents and her fear of her identification with them. Medea appeared to be comforting her children, but in fact she had murdered them. Blood dripped from their slit throats. While she identified with Medea, Nancy also was the murdered child, with blood dripping from her vagina. She also connected this dream to her sibling rivalry, which shed further light on her fears of murdering her son, her compulsive need to hide her kitchen knives, and her obsessive worry about her own child's safety. In her mind, sex and violence, rape and murder were fused around the terror and pain of the incestuous act.

As Nancy became increasingly conscious of her aggressive identification with her father, her appearance became more masculine. She dressed in blue jeans and large blouses and wore flat shoes and short hair. During this phase of treatment, she dreamed of being frightened by a lion, but then remaining with the lion and taming him to the point of being able to pat the lion without fear. In response to this dream, she associated not only to her father's penis, but to the lion's roar within her, the phallic, assertive, energetic, stubborn side of herself. At the height of this phase, she dreamed of drowning her son and accepted my interpretation that she was trying to drown the boy within her. She responded by talking about her similarity to her young son and her belief that her parents wished that she had been born a boy.

Further work revealed that Nancy felt more powerful and protected by the fantasy of having a penis. Nancy recalled that even before her mother abandoned her, she had used a toilet paper roll to pretend she had a penis, with which she imagined making love to her sister. (I speculated silently that this fantasy may have reflected an additional trauma, that of early primal scene exposure, which predated and further paved the way for the incest. However, data to support this speculation was never produced.) Associating to my sitting behind the analytic couch, Nancy remembered that her father had entered her from behind on the first occasion of the incest. She identified with me as the aggressive father /analyst behind her and dreamed of herself with a penis, making love to me from behind. She also associated this dream to the Medea fantasy—the possession of the penis made her the mother with the knife.

Ultimately, the awareness of her identification with the male aggressor and of her hatred of that part of herself allowed Nancy to accept and integrate herself as a woman. No longer afraid of being like her father, she devoted more time to mothering her son. His tantrums ceased, as he felt closer to his now more affectionate mother.

Her obsessions became less violent after 18 months. Rather than picturing her child in a terrible accident, she had thoughts like "M stands for murder as well as mother." These obsessions felt like "a punch in the uterus," because they spoiled her pleasure with her son. Her dreams, too, revealed more displaced symbols and were less frightening. For example, when dreaming of the damage caused by the incest, she now dreamed that she wore a low-cut, sequined dress that showed off her defects—a curvature of the spine and a protruding, pregnantlike abdomen. She felt her desire to be feminine and feared that to be a woman meant to be defective. She wished to run away from this conflict, as her mother had run from hers. She dreamed of missing a session and going for a drive in a low-slung, phallic-shaped sports car.

As the trauma of the incest and her loss of mother were worked through, her dreams reflected her newly developing desires for femininity. For example, in dream, she told a friend not to touch a lovely bowl of precariously stacked, round fruit covered with an intricate design. She associated the design with her own intricate genitalia. For many years well into her adulthood, she had not been aware of her how genitalia looked and had not known where her clitoris was. She grieved over the years of her sexual inhibition and remembered her mother's prohibition against masturbation. She recognized sexual excitement during the analytic hour and wondered how she could manage to be close to her women friends without feeling sexually aroused.

During the final year of analysis, Nancy resolved many of her conflicts about being a woman. She did not want to be a defeated victim like her mother or herself as a little girl. She felt as though she were the personification of her mother's rage at her father. She yearned for an identification with another woman, one who could be confident and strong and still be sexual. She then became curious about my sex life. Was I orgasmic? Did I have affairs? She identified with her idealized image of me, and her style of dress changed to soft, feminine, and elegant. She noted our similarity of hair and eye colors and wore clothing that was the color of my clothing. Nancy read novels by strong women authors, like Jane Austen and Virginia Wolfe. She also formed many close friendships with successful, bright women and enjoyed telling me stories about their successes.

Through a series of dreams, she expressed greater comfort with her vagina. She dreamt of having an "opening" in an art gallery with paintings of lovely swirling holes. She associated this dream to her wish to show her husband her sexual excitement. She dreamed that the walls of my office were covered with soft, pink material and associated to the walls of her vagina. She reported that she could now feel the inside of her vagina when making love with her husband, and love making had become more satisfying.

Having worked through the consequences of the incest and many of the conflicts to which it had given rise and having consolidated her sense of herself as a positive, feminine, sexually competent mature woman, Nancy now seemed able to deal more effectively with the usual oedipal and preoedipal conflicts and transferences. She could now face her fears of competing with her mother. For example, she recalled being frightened that her mother would find out about the incest and want to kill her. She flirted openly with her friends' husbands and now recognized her compulsion to do so. She felt my interpretations as competitive and wondered if I was jealous of her buying a new home. She noted that she enjoyed competing with her girl-friends and also recognized her competition with her husband and me.

During this period, Nancy also recognized her dependency on me in the maternal transference and dreamed of herself as a nine-year-old girl, waiting to go into my child consultation office, while I played with another little girl. In the dream, her old therapist appeared to tell her that I would soon be finished and she could then play with me. She associated from this dream to her mother's caring for her younger sisters. Through our "playing" with her associations in her analysis, I became the mother who played with her before the incest and the abandonment. Through the analysis of the dream, Nancy, realizing that she had tried to deal with her feelings about the birth of her sisters by pretending to be a big girl, could now be in touch with her transference longings to be comforted. She imagined that I would hold her as her husband did and dreamed of visiting her childhood home and rediscovering the playful mother who had existed for her before abandoning her at age 5. In her life and in her analysis, she also rediscovered her ability to play, to fantasize, and to dream in ways that helped her to work through her conflicts.

After three years of analysis and ready for termination, Nancy dreamed of leaving me. In the dream, she was a little girl, holding a suitcase—her identification with me—and waiting for the train. She remembered for the first time that her mother had carried a suitcase when she left. She then dreamed of traveling in a caravan of protected, covered wagons with other strong women. She snuggled in the driver's seat with her strong, competent mother. Associating to this dream, she remembered that she had enjoyed sleeping with her mother and sisters.

A dream at the end of Nancy's analysis illustrated her increased ability to use symbols with displacement and secondary elaboration. In it, she was on a boat with children and there was "damage below." The iron hatch cover, which protected her, also prevented her escape. She opened the hatch to escape, leaving the children behind. In her associations, it was clear that in leaving analysis, she was leaving behind her childhood and the pain and suffering she had endured. She was now free. The warm water reminded her of swimming with father in a warm lake, years before the incest. He held her in the water as he taught her to swim. Somehow, remembering these pleasant memories of her father before the incest allowed her to be sexually freer with her husband.

In a final dream, Nancy refused to act in the Medea drama, saying that she could not even pretend such a dreadful act as killing her own children. I pointed out to her that now she could choose. She did not have to identify with her flawed parents, who had acted in such a way. Nancy could now play with the symbol "act"—act in a play, the act of a play, and acting as action and as identification.

By the end of the treatment, Nancy felt pleased with her life. The scar of the incest remained, but she was much less haunted by her past. She loved her husband very much, and they shared a wonderful, sexually intimate vacation. She still had difficulty having orgasm during intercourse but had orgasms more easily with petting and masturbation. She enjoyed her friends, her son, and her work. She enjoyed being a woman.

DISCUSSION

The consequences and meaning of the experience of incest, while certainly traumatic in any case, will vary with the individual and reflect the age at which it occurred, the pretraumatic object relationships and levels of development, the family role and relationship of the incestuous object, and the child's posttraumatic experiences. In particular, the level of ego development at the time of trauma is critical. Krystal (1978) discusses this point and suggests that a crucial turning point in the child's ability to handle trauma occurs around the age of five (that is, the beginning of the resolution of the oedipal period). At that time, children have the potential to attain and consolidate the capacity to identify with the parent in handling and tolerating affect. When her mother left Nancy had reached a level of ego development consistent with the oedipal period. She struggled to function separately from her mother, remembered enjoying being with her father, and reacted to the mother's departure by attempting to be more grown up and disdaining her sisters' infantile behavior. Thus, although her ego was severely stressed by this first trauma, Nancy had sufficient internal reserves and outer resources to handle it mostly by defenses and symptom formation rather than by structural disorganization and severe ego distortions.

After the incest, however, Nancy, responded by splitting off her affective response, severely inhibiting her ego development, numbing her sexual feelings, and constricting her cognitive field and use of fantasy, play, and symbols, especially in regard to aggression and conflicts and memories related to the incest. Thus, she reported feeling numb, guilty, and scared, as she was continually encountering frightening memory fragments and feelings that reminded her of the incest.

One consequence of the incest trauma for Nancy was the disruption of her symbolizing capacities as reflected in her fantasies, play, and dream life. In describing a very different kind of trauma, that occurring in adult children of concentration camp survivors, Gubrich-Simitis (1984) described a similar kind of distortion. She noted that her patients demonstrated a cognitive constriction in the use of metaphors, which limited their ability to deal effectively with sexual and aggressive conflicts (p. 305). In children of survivors of the Holocaust and in patients like Nancy who were subjected to incest during latency, the mechanism involved appears to be an intense repression of the connections between the symbol and the real meaning, or real object, that it might come to represent.

Nancy had developed the ability to use fantasy and symbols before her mother abandoned her. For example, she dealt with her rage at the birth of a sibling by putting the doll in the street to be run over by a truck. However, she recalled less interest in play after her mother's return. Fantasy made her too anxious. The incest produced overwhelming sexual and aggressive stimulation and destroyed the protective shield derived from her relationship with her grandmother and father. She was left alone with her angry and sexual feelings and feared being overwhelmed by them. The result was a further inhibition of fantasy and symbolization.

Developmentally speaking, the ability to protect oneself from overwhelming affect is associated with primary object relationships. A competent parenting figure will provide a child with an identificatory model for managing affective responses and will function through caretaking activities as the child's protector from overwhelming stimuli. In the latter capacity, the primary object acts as an auxiliary stimulus barrier, a protective shield, who comforts the child so that the child is not overwhelmed by her own emotions. When this protective function fails, intense stimuli can result in traumatic affects, causing the child not only to feel helpless, but also to feel the absence or loss of the protective parental object.

In the analysis of those patients for whom this protective

parental function has miscarried, the analyst's providing the protection needed for the development of a therapeutic alliance and positive transference is complicated and difficult. The double loss of the protective father and the mother in the case of father–daughter incest deprives the patient not only of her parents, but also of the ability to form future trusting relationships, including that with the analyst. For the patient, the transference may recreate the feelings of seduction, betrayal, and lack of protection that she experienced in childhood and has reexperienced constantly since then at the hands of her internalized parents and their external surrogates. Thus, in the experience of the patient, the analyst becomes both the perpetrator and the potential protector in the transference, making the positive transference and the alliance difficult to maintain under the siege of transference feelings of distrust, betrayal, and seduction. In such cases, the symbolic recreation of the lost protective parental function in the analytic setting is a precondition for therapeutic success. As I believe Nancy's analysis shows, this symbolic provision of a restored protective function can enable a patient to regain a greater use of symbols in fantasy and dreams, thereby allowing her to work through the conflicts that such trauma as abandonment and incest have produced.

Following the course of her dream life, one is able to see how the restoration of the function of symbols and fantasies mirrored and contributed to Nancy's recovery. The preanalytic dreams were realistic, concrete, and frightening and elicited no associations except to the actual act of incest. Nancy was either overwhelmed by her feelings and associations to the incest, as expressed in her panic attacks, or else she distanced herself by being objective, an "over the fence" defense, as expressed in her opening analytic dream. She also distanced herself from her son, who responded with temper tantrums in an attempt to be close to her, and from her husband, with whom she was frigid and critical. Similarly, she avoided a close emotional connection with me during her psychotherapy. Her dreams about the dam and road block signaled the beginnings of her gaining some protection from her feelings about the incest and abandonment.

While a sense of safety in the analytic relationship was being established, the therapeutic alliance and positive transference could deepen. Nancy's dreams then began to show an increasing accessibility and richness in their associative connections. Through symbols, Nancy could now experience both parts of a conflict. For example, in the Medea dream, she was able to see that she was both victim and murderer. As she recognized her identification with her murderer/father and her desire for revenge, she no longer had to manage her aggression by obsessive concerns for her son's safety or by compulsively putting away knives. She could see that her fear of being the murderer came from her own fear of being murdered, slit open, by her father's penis/knife. The knife symbol itself became modified, as reflected in the dream about the lion. Here again, both aspects of the lion could be experienced. The lion was dangerous, but could also be made a friend. Thus, Nancy came to enjoy her husband's masculinity, his penis, as well as the lion within her—her early identification with father and her own suppressed, energetic, lively little girl self.

As Nancy's conflicts were analyzed, she regained her ability to play. She played with her son, played with symbols in her dreams and within the analysis and, through the dream of waiting to play with me in my child consultation office, remembered playing with her mother. In one of her final dreams, she was able to displace and symbolize the incest and its damage from herself to a boat, from which she could "escape" by swimming, an activity she had learned from father prior to the incest.

The unconscious meaning of the incest to Nancy was to feel herself as "damaged below." Her genitals, her uterus, were ripped. Her sex life and her ability to mother were impaired. The restoration of the damage prior to her analysis was to identify with the male aggressor, which further served to conflict her feminine identity. Katan (1973), in her article on children who had been raped and later treated when they were adults, reported several cases of women who felt as though they had acquired a penis. Nancy, too, unconsciously restored the fantasied penis that she had as a three-year-old playing with her sister. This fantasy protected her against feeling helpless and damaged but produced great conflicts in her feminine identity. The resolution of this conflict came as she acknowledged and analyzed her rage toward her father, gave up her defensive identification with him as aggressor and seducer, and positively identified with the strong, feminine analyst, who represented the mother before the abandonment.

Thus, for Nancy, psychoanalysis provided the sanitary pad, the bandage for her vaginal wound, caused by her father's penis ripping her genitals during the act of intercourse, that she longed for in her dream. Through effective conflict resolution brought about by the analytic work, her ego capacity to use symbols, fantasy and play freely was reclaimed and important associative connections between the events and conflicts produced by the incest were restored. With the symbols found in her dreams and fantasies, Nancy could then work through much of the damage done by the incest. She was no longer frightened, numbed, and guilty. She grieved for the loss of her parents—the father through incest and the mother through the inital abandonment and failure to protect her from the father. She relinquished her identification with the father as the aggressor and achieved a better resolution of the resulting conflicts that affected her roles as wife, mother, and woman. She no longer feared being Medea, the vengeful murderer, and regaining access to earlier identifications with kind, loving, effective parents, could remember her parents before the abandonment and incest.

REFERENCES

DeSaussiere, J. (1982), Dreams and dreaming in relation to trauma in childhood, *Internat. J. Psycho-Anal*, 63:167–176.

Dowling, S., (1987), The interpretation of dreams in the reconstruction of trauma. In: The *Interpretations of Dreams in Clinical Work*, ed. A. Rothstein, Madison, CT: International Universities Press, pp. 47–56.

Freud, S. (1926), Inhibition, symptoms and anxiety. *Standard Edition*, 20:87- 172. London: Hogarth Press, 1959.

Grubrich-Simitis, I. (1984), From concretism to metaphor: Thoughts on some theoretical and technical aspects of the psychoanalytic work with children of holocaust survivors. *The Psychoanalytic Study of the Child*, 39:301–320. New Haven, CT: Yale University Press.

Herman, J. (1981), *Father–Daughter Incest*. Cambridge, MA: Harvard University Press.

Katan, A. (1973), Children who were raped. *The Psychoanalytic Study of the Child*, 28:208–224. New Haven, CT: Yale University Press.

Krystal, H. (1978), Trauma and affects. *The Psychoanalytic Study of the Child,* 33:81–116. New Haven, CT: Yale University Press.

LaPlanche, J. & Pontalis, J.B. (1973), *The Language of Psychoanalysis.* New York: Norton.

Sarnoff, C. (1976), *Latency* New York: Aronson.

8

Countertransference in the Analysis of an Adult Who Was Sexually Abused as a Child

Nydia Lisman-Pieczanski

During the psychoanalytic treatment of a woman who was sexually abused in her childhood by her godfather, feelings of deadness, disillusionment, helplessness, and disbelief, emerged in the countertransference with unusual strength. In discussion with colleagues, I found that they too had experienced similar reactions to such patients. In this chapter, I will present data from the analytic process with a focus on the consequences of the childhood sexual abuse and its implications for the counter-transference.

Freud (1910) first described countertransference as the emotional response of the analyst to stimuli coming from the patient, the result of the influence of the patient on the unconscious feelings of the analyst. Freud considered countertransference an obstacle to the unfolding of the therapeutic process.

Eighty years later, it is increasingly clear that countertransference also contains fundamental clues for the understanding of some of the basic ingredients of the patient's psychic world. In my own view, transference and countertransference are intimately linked as part of the emotional experience that is unique to each analyst–analyzand couple.

In the case that I will describe memories related to the sexual abuse emerged as a result of reconstruction during the analysis. The accuracy of the recovered memories was later confirmed by an older sister. It is my contention that these repressed traumatic experiences became part and parcel of the patient's inner world, determining the main features of her relationships. She belonged to a world ruled by a "culture of abuse." She felt that she existed only insofar as she could define herself and others with respect to the abuse. Consequently, it was very natural for her to "understand" her role in the analysis and my interpretations as part of a process in which a helpless child was constantly being abused. The identity of the victim varied. Sometimes, it was the patient; other times, it was I.

FIRST ENCOUNTER

Ms. S was a 35-year-old psychotherapist who initially came to me seeking supervision of her clinical work. During our first hour together she presented the case of a female physician who had begun therapy because she was unable to conceive. The treatment that Ms. S reported was successful to the extent that her patient did in fact become pregnant. However, her patient discontinued the therapy immediately after the birth of the child, leaving Ms. S feeling abused, and taken for granted.

At the end of the first hour Ms. S announced that she was actually looking for an analyst and asked me to take her on in treatment. She added that she had used the supervisory hour to explore my psychoanalytic approach and, having decided that I was a "real" Kleinian, felt that I was the "right" person to take care of her.

This highly unusual approach to seeking analysis took me by surprise and awakened my interest and curiosity. I worried that, should I treat her, I might be violating some fundamental analytic principle—as if we were involved in some perverse acting-out. Although the quality and intensity of my emotional response was unusual for me, I suggested that we suspend supervision and begin a series of consultative interviews. When she left that first hour I realized that my initial countertransference reaction also included a fear of losing my bearings and a fantasy of becoming, as it were, a confused infant, rejected by my analytic parents for breaking the law.

I used my response to her unusual presentation and the supervisory meeting as part of the diagnostic process. I felt that she had powerfully communicated to me that, as her analyst, I would have to deal with painful confusion, violation of some basic rules, and extreme suspicion of any dependent relationship. I thought of my countertransference as the result of her intense projective defense mechanisms. My state of mind probably reflected how her infantile self reacted, and still reacts, to contact with certain parental imagos.

CLINICAL ASSESSMENT

Ms. S told me that she had been having an affair for about three years with a psychiatrist, Dr. R, who had seen her in psychodynamic psychotherapy for two years. He was 20 years older than she. Eventually their treatment came to an end when they became lovers. After three years, during which they lived together, she decided to leave him. The relationship seemed to have no future. Ms. S felt that his lack of committment to her "forced" her to leave him.

Now she needed my help to reorganize her personal and professional life, which was in a state of complete chaos. After the separation, she was unable to work because Dr. R was her sole source of referrals. Furthermore, her only other source of income—a small property she had inherited from her father—had to be sold to pay overdue taxes. In the end she went to live in a small, run-down room for six months and applied for a position in a psychiatric hospital. Soon after she began to take some private cases, she moved to a small, expensive apartment. She could not see that with her limited financial resources she would again very shortly find herself in trouble.

Ms. S was the youngest of four children born to a family of inmigrants. She had two brothers and a sister. The elder brother, like her father, had never adjusted to the new country. Neither learned the language. Ms. S's younger brother had a university degree. She recalls that when she was 10 years old she was afraid of staying alone with him for any length of time, feeling claustrophobic or on the verge of fainting. Her sister is married and has two children.

Ms. S's parents came from very different socioeconomic backgrounds. Mother was of humble origins, while father belonged to a cultured, middle-class family. Her paternal grandfather had disappeared when father was a child. At age 18 father discovered that his true (biological) father had been the "uncle" who helped look after him until father married. Ms. S reported that this illegitimate pregnancy was the cause of her paternal grandmother's leading a socially isolated and secluded life. Ms. S had been led to think that her grandfather had abandoned the family owing to a financial crisis.

As we can see, concealment and what I call "twisting of the truth" were constantly present in her life. By twisting of the truth I mean a distortion of reality, (internal and external), aimed at draining away the original meaning of a relationship. The new, twisted version is always more exciting, and less painful, removing all awareness of smallness and dependence.

Ms. S described her mother as a hard worker; her father, as tyrannical and mean spirited. For example, father refused to pay for the funeral of her maternal grandparents, who were finally buried in a common grave for the destitute. This event remained for mother a source of interminable rage and resentment.

Because of their impoverished circumstances, Ms. S's father left his wife and family, including the two-year-old Ms. S behind in Europe while he resettled in South America. During this period, her mother was depressed, and overwhelmed by poverty. The family was reunited when Ms. S was three years old. These were difficult times for the S's, and Ms. S had to share a bed with her parents.

During those early years in South America the S family established a close relationship with a native man slightly older than Ms. S's eldest brother (15 years her senior). He was their next door neighbor and worked in the family business, a small carpenter's workshop. This young man, who later became my patient's godfather, played an integral role as the S family's link with their new country and represented an idealized male identity.

When she was 17 years old, Ms. S was working for her godfather in his office when he attempted to seduce her. Although, in retrospect, his advances were blatant, she was not then clear about his intentions. Soon thereafter she went abroad to further her education. Even in the light of her later maturity, Ms. S had no sense that her sudden departure might have been linked to her godfather's advances. She had left for Europe against her father's wishes, and it was there that she learned of father's death. The news came to her several months after the event, and she reacted with a physical collapse that necessitated her hospitalization. According to her medical report, the doctors could not agree on a diagnosis and told her that she was having a psychotic breakdown. But rather than offer her treatment there, they advised her to return home, which she did.

Upon her return she began psychotherapy, and improved to the extent that she could continue her education, obtaining a degree in psychology. Although she did well academically, she drifted into impulsive, superficial, and perverse relationships. In retrospect, this behavior belonged to the crystalization of the unconscious fantasies that had fueled her behavior since childhood.

Ms. S never forgave her family for not telling her of her father's illness. Her memories remained centered on how neglected he had been by the family and by his doctors. She felt that father had died in poverty and neglect as part of mother's "vendetta" for what he had done to her parents (Ms. S's maternal grandparents) a generation earlier.

Her descriptions of her sexual life were tinged with much resentment and bitterness. She complained that female identity implied dependency, and that meant being a loser. For a significant part of her sexual life she was frigid. Only her partners enjoyed sex, while she felt she was a "provider of orgasms."

After her return from Europe, she had had several relationships in which she was frigid, until she started a bisexual relationship with a man and a woman much older than herself. It did not last long, and eventually she became the exclusive partner of the man, got pregnant, and aborted without her partner's knowledge. When she ended the pregnancy, she "aborted" the relationship, confident that she had finally overcome her frigidity.

This relationship was followed by brief affairs until she met

Dr. R. With him, intercourse was "satisfactory." During her analysis she told me the following about the relationship: "I gave him my sexuality, my money, and my youth, but he would not commit himself."

THE TREATMENT

For the first 18 months of the analysis, Ms. S was aggressive, agitated, and always angry because of some injustice or abuse of which she had been the victim. She was sometimes very paranoid and almost deluded, unable to be in touch with either internal or external reality. She could also be an intelligent and attractive human being. These variations in her behavior created countertransference feelings of unpredictability and surprise. Most unexpectedly we could start off on a string of good sessions, characterized by increasing awareness and sustained insight. Equally unexpectedly, this process could at any time come to an abrupt stop, and the analytic dialogue would consist of associations relating to the collapse of the treatment.

I slowly began to understand these oscillations as a defensive system aimed at preventing closeness with some very painful parts of her inner world. She had to avoid the experience of anguished dependence and need. To be in touch with those aspects of her mind made her feel like a hopeless orphan that anyone could take advantage of.

Her mental ups and downs were frequently accompanied by somatic reactions. For example, before analytic breaks, she would grow increasingly pale and lose weight. During those sessions I became really worried about her, particularly because she seemed to be totally oblivious of what was taking place. In fact, she thought I was the one that lost weight. This was a characteristic transference-countertransference experience, the product of an interaction in which projective mechanisms were predominant in her mental functioning. It resulted in her perception of me, as a "useless, empty person."

THE FIRST DREAM

At the end of the second year of analysis Ms. S reported a dream in which she was lying on her back, blinded by a powerful light that gave her a feeling of relief. She felt the dream was a memory of something she could not identify. She associated the light with a feeling of fascination. Her godfather's room had had a very powerful lightbulb. While telling me this, she became anxious and agitated. She continued with a description of the room. It had a bed, and she could "see" herself as a young child lying on the bed looking at the light. She started crying and described how her godfather masturbated her while she looked at the blinding light. This revealing dream made her feel panic as she made contact with an experience in which pleasure and violence came together. Ms. S. had completely repressed this memory until she had the dream. Further analysis of the dream showed that the dynamic function of the light was to eliminate the traumatic memory from her mind. Light, a sensory perception, comforted her by blinding. It was a perverse light, which did not enlighten. It hid the outrage that had been committed on her infant self.

Ms. S discussed the content of her recovered memories with her sister, partly to determine whether the events had really taken place. The sister confirmed the memories, adding that the last time my patient had been left alone with her godfather the sister had found her almost unconscious after he had tried to penetrate her at the age of six and a half. Neither the patient nor her sister had told their parents about the sexual abuse. However, for no other apparent reason, mother suddenly discontinued her job for a year, until, when Ms. S was seven years old, they moved to another house. After that time, my patient saw her godfather only on her birthdays, until she started to work for him at the age of 17.

THE SECOND DREAM

Several months after this first dream, Ms. S dreamed that I had had a car accident in which I nearly died. I had been stunned and lay on a sofa. I had avoided "irreversible" death by becoming immobile and passive. Instead, I had felt pleasure and relief.

The analysis of this dream showed that immobility, passivity, and "near deathness" defended her against a catastrophic experience. These defenses were the functional equivalents of blindness in the first dream. The car in the dream represented her own body. As in the real event, in which she did not look at her body while she was masturbated by her godfather, we could not see the damaged car in the dream. Similarly, my life-saving passivity and immobility mirrored her childhood response to the sexual assault

THE END OF THE ANALYSIS

At the end of the third year of analysis Ms. S learned that Dr. R, the psychiatrist with whom she had had an affair, had cancer. Coincidentally this occurred when her analysis was again threatened by interruption due to financial difficulties. Faced with the prospect of Dr. R's death and the loss of her analysis, she suffered another physical collapse and was taken to hospital. A week later she telephoned to say that she was resuming treatment. The following Monday she came back looking healthy and full of vitality. These sudden, unexpected shifts left me feeling unreal, as if I had lost track of her psychic evolution.

Subsequently, her newly regained vitality proved short-lived. She had an unstoppable professional, social, and financial breakdown. I tried to continue treating her for a few months without charging for the sessions. However, she soon decided to discontinue the analysis because she felt it was a "brutal abuse" for me to continue to see her.

DISCUSSION

The analysis of Ms. S showed the extent to which her psychic structure was organized around a combination of precoscious sexual overexcitement, emotional neglect by parental objects, and sexual abuse. On this foundation she developed her basic patterns of personal relationships, frequently becoming identified with the neglectful and abusive parent. Her sexual overexcitement had started well before she met her godfather, at the

time when she shared a bed with her parents. It was preceded by
the financial and emotional impoverishment produced when her
father left the family behind to settle in South America and her
mother became severely depressed.

In attempting to treat patients like Ms. S, we are faced with the
challenge of helping people whose inner world is populated by
parental imagos linked with neglect, violence, and disregard for
their infantile needs. The result of such disordered internal
object relationships is a constant, unconscious pressure to turn
the analysis into a sadomasochistic experience; a kind of painful
"mating" that is acted out in the transference. For example, Ms.
S would announce at the beginning of the session that she had
brought the money to pay for her analysis. But when the session
was over she would stand up and walk out without paying the
bill, leaving me in a state of frustration. I could not stop myself
from staring at her handbag. Thus, she reproduced in my
countertransference the experience of the blinding fascination: I
would passively stare at the bag, as she had looked at the light,
paralyzed, speechless, and needy. I was put in the position of
the helpless baby, abused by maternal deprivation and the
godfather's assault and having feelings of rage and impotence. I
had to recover myself and try to put into words this violent
emotional interaction.

The defense mechanisms involved in the foregoing example
are of a very primitive kind. Projective identification, a defense
that by its very nature completely disrupts insight, predominates
(Klein, 1946). Contact with these patients, deeply affects the
therapist's inner balance and capacity to understand and care.
Thus, the analytic process, frequently includes the analyst's
cyclic attempts to rescue his or her analytic capacity.

At the same time, the countertransference feelings, stirred up
by projective identification, constitute a unique source of information about the patient's inner world and unconscious phantasies. I have tried to describe some of the difficult moments I
had to endure and the troubles I had in extricating myself from
the emotional atmosphere created by the more deprived and
anguished aspects of my patient. I am sure that some of my
countertransference was a reproduction of Ms. S's unconscious
fantasies in my mind. In other words, those extremely painful

moments of doubt, frustration, helplessness, and mental blindness were the only way she had of letting me know how it felt to be in her predicament.

Ms. S's case is very similar to those described by Joseph (1982). Her patients also found themselves compelled to take their relationships to the verge of a breakdown, to a "near-death" state. Like Ms. S's, their destructiveness was directed to their bodies as well as to their psyches.

Ms. S's destructive attitudes toward her external and internal world, including constant attacks on her body, usually stirred up guilt in my countertransference, as I expected myself to be more effective in stopping her from being so self-destructive. I think that this situation reflects a kind of addiction Ms. S had to a relationship hinging on omnipotent fantasies felt as a promise of well-being but based on lies and delusional beliefs.

The root of such addictive problems lies in profound alterations of the earliest object relationships. Bick (1968) describes children who in early contact with their mothers fail to internalize a holding function. This failure leads to an inability to form a "psychic skin" to "hold" them together. She describes responses to separation similar to those that I found in my patient. Bick's patients felt separation as a "tearing apart." Interestingly, the images dreamed by Ms. S, in which she looked at the dazzling, blinding light, are similar to Bick's description of babies and very disturbed children who focus on bright objects, light, and sounds. Bick suggests that the meaning of this experience is to eliminate the threat of death or disintegration from their mental apparatus.

Under normal circumstances, the violence and sadism present in early instinctual life are neutralized by love and adequate parental responses. My patient's deeply disrupted early relationships left her without an adequate buffer, abnormally exposed to the disintegrating effects of her own instinctual life. This failure of the parental containing function (Bion, 1962) severely distorted and limited her early development and contributed to the production of a vulnerable ego, addictively entangled in hopeless experiences.

As Ms. S's analyst, I had to work through my own strong feelings, including deadness, irritation, outrage, and hopelessness, which resulted from my becoming enmeshed in archaic relationships. I had to learn to tolerate, understand, and, when possible, communicate to the patient, in the form of an interpretation, the meaning of what I was feeling.

The impact of severely disturbed patients on the analyst can not and should not be avoided, nor should it be. As Brenman-Pick (1985) explains, patients are "consciously or unconsciously mindful as to whether the analyst evades or meets the issues. The contention that the analyst is not affected by these experiences is both false and would convey to the patient that his plight, pain and behaviour are emotionally ignored by the analyst" (p. 165). In other words, analysts must work to transform their own emotional experience in the countertransference into understanding. If they cannot succeed in this endeavor, they cannot expect their patients to do so either.

REFERENCES

Bick, E. (1968), The experience of skin in early object relations. *Internat. J. Psycho-Anal.*, 49:484–486.

Bion, W. (1962), *Learning from Experience*. London: Heinemann.

Brenman-Pick, I. (1985), Working through in the countertransference. *Internat. J. Psycho-Anal.* 66:157–166.

Freud, S. (1910), Future perspectives in psychoanalytic therapy. *Standard Edition*, 11:139–151. London; Hogarth Press, 1957.

Joseph, B. (1982), Addiction to near death, *Internat. J. Psycho-Anal.*, 63:449–456.

9 Residues of Incest

Selma Kramer

During the past 20 years, there has been an increasing number of published reports on the psychoanalytic treatment of children and adults who experienced maternal or paternal incest during their childhood or adolescence. Still, relatively few authors seem to concern themselves with reports of such psychoanalyses. In the main, they have been Shengold (1967, 1974, 1979, 1980), who reported physical, sexual, and psychological abuse by parents as "soul murder" of their children; Margolis (1977, 1984), who wrote about consummated incest in an adolescent male; Silber (1979); and Kramer (1974, 1980, 1985, 1987), who wrote about maternal incest and its treatment.

In this chapter, I continue my exploration of the long-term consequences of incest by examining two phenomena that I believe are the residues of parental sexual abuse. The first phenomenon is the varieties of physical sensation and disturbances in sexual functioning that I call "somatic memories." The second is the general and specific learning problems that patients who were incestuously involved with their parents often demonstrate. As background to my discussion, I shall begin by briefly reviewing some relevant conclusions drawn from previous work with this population of patients.

While sexual abuse in childhood is apt to be disturbing for the child's development independent of whether the abuser is a stranger or a family member, incest is particularly disruptive when committed by a parent. In such instances, the child easily loses the capacity to trust authority figures. In addition, the sense of guilt and responsibility for the act, which the child is apt to feel by virtue of its self-centered cognitive orientation, is reinforced by at least two additional factors. The first relates to the child's sensitivity to the parent's role as arbiter of right and wrong, which makes the child particularly susceptible to any remarks or behavior of the abusing parents intended to induce or reinforce a sense of guilt in the child. (Of particular relevance here is the process by which the abusing parent forces his or her own sense of guilt into the child, as was first described by Ferenczi in 1933). The second factor promoting guilt is that the excitement arising from the sexual act is occurring with an object who is still tinged with unresolved oedipal feelings and hence is particularly forbidden.

Within this range of general response to parental incest are important differences that result from whether the incestuous parent is the mother or the father. It has been my experience that mothers who engage in incest with their children have more serious psychopathology than do fathers who commit incest. In addition—or possibly as a consequence—the child, who is often the product of an unwanted pregnancy, is considered by the mother to be unrewarding and imperfect, as often turns out to be how the mother felt herself to be perceived and treated by her own mother.

In the cases of mother–child incest that I have treated, the sexual abuse started early as an outgrowth of the mothers' too zealous attention to the hygiene of their children's peritoneal areas. The "cleansing" continued for much too long and was converted by the mothers into masturbation of their children. Two of my patients, Donald (Kramer, 1974) and Casey (Kramer, 1980) stopped their mothers from doing this only when they reached adolescence and began to fear that their mother's attentions would produce orgasm. The abuse of a third patient, Abby (Kramer, 1980), stopped only after the child had been brought to treatment. I have come to believe that because the abuse started so early and was perpetrated by their mothers, at a time when they were at the center of their children's universe, the consequences for these children were extensive and severe, leading to the particular disturbance in reality testing that underlies what I have termed "object coercive doubting" (Kramer, 1985).

In contrast, fathers are seldom sexually abusive until the child is well into latency or adolescence. The later onset means that the child's reality testing is usually much better established and will therefore be significantly less affected by the incest and its consequences than in those instances where the sexual abuser was the mother and the incest began much earlier. The constellation of residues that I wish to focus on here, however, is one that I have found in patients of both sexes who were incestuously involved with either mother or father. The most noteworthy constellation I refer to as "somatic memories" of incest. These are bodily sensations that occur well into adulthood and are most often accompanied by great displeasure, aversion, or physical pain during foreplay, intromission, or coitus. Occasionally, in contrast to hyperesthesia, these patients reported reacting to touch in the opposite way, with muted feelings, frigidity, and anorgasmia. Some patients reported feeling furious during lovemaking, a fury that was at first incomprehensible, especially when they considered that they themselves had either initiated or consented to the sexual overtures. In their sessions, these patients experienced and complained of hyperacusis, hyperosmia, and sensitivity to touch (e.g., my couch was "scratchy"). One patient feared strangers whom she might encounter on the way to the office and was afraid that I would allow a stranger to touch her body.

Steele (personal communication) agreed that somatic sensitivity and other sexual problems in adults may derive from childhood sexual abuse. Steele's views are consonant with those of Katan (1973), who also noted that her patients had problems in integrating libidinal and aggressive drives and frequently turned their aggressions against themselves.

Frequently interrelated with the somatic memories are problems in learning, in retaining what has been learned, and in "showing what one knows"—e.g., by reciting in school, doing well on tests, and the like. These patients may also demonstrate muting of their affects, as well as problems in perceiving affects in themselves or in others. At times, this muting of affects may progress to a picture not unlike that of a clinical depression.

None of my patients initially told me that incest had occurred. Most did not remember. In fact, one patient had amnesia for the first eight years of her life. As treatment progressed and memories of the incest became available, they were tolerated by means of intermittent denial, disavowal, or splitting. Reconstruction was necessary in every case to represent to the patient the story he or she had told me but could not really perceive or accept. Reconstruction also verified the patient's reality, in contrast to the parental denial of the incest. The somatic memories represent, I feel, a breakthrough caused by incomplete repression.

CLINICAL EXAMPLES

Case #1

Casey came to analysis at age 20 because she "did not know where to go in life." She had trained for ballet, but now, although she had been told she had a successful career ahead of her, she found it impossible to become a professional dancer. She "froze up" on the stage and could not tolerate being touched or, especially, lifted by her partner. She also feared performing in public; she would become confused and forget her routine. It soon became obvious in the analysis that she feared that being successful would mean leaving home.

Casey was the younger of two sisters; there was also a brother ten years younger. Her mother had not wanted to be pregnant with Casey, but when the pregnancy was accepted, the mother wished for a boy. Instead, she gave birth to a girl with a minor birth defect. Casey and her mother had been overly close, "enmeshed." She manifested splitting of the self and maternal object representations, which succeeded in Casey's retaining a "good" representation of her mother, relegating "badness" to teachers, onto whom all evil was placed. The self was "good," nonhostile, noncompetitive, nonsexy; her peers, whom she envied but could not relate to, were "bad." Only after the two sides of self and object were fused could she remember what she

had known but could not let herself acknowledge or tell me—
that her mother, as far back as Casey could remember, had
masturbated her until she reached puberty. Even now Casey had
to stop her mother from touching her clothed body. Casey's
analysis was slow and, to her, distressing, for it meant that she
had to see things in her mother that were painful to see. She was
reluctant to forego the security of allowing her mother to make
plans for her, to comfort her when Casey was troubled, to spend
money on her. For a long time the analysis and the analyst were
the intruders, threatening the sanctity of the distorted mother–
child relationship. More than once Casey blurted out, "You
want me to become independent, to give up what I count on!" At
the same time she felt that I was as seductive as was her mother
because I encouraged free association, which in Casey's mind,
was something dirty and bad. Only when the actual seduction
and its vicissitudes had been analyzed could Casey go through
the development process necessary for her to be a separate and
appropriately sexual individual.

Casey had suffered a severe narcissistic injury as a result of her
mother's use of Casey's genitals as a dehumanized part of herself
and also because of her mother's frequent rejection of Casey.
This intrusion interfered greatly with Casey's early development
and made her question the "ownership of her body" (Laufer,
1968, p. 115).

Casey lacked a healthy sense of autonomy and self-worth.
Instead, she was plagued by self-doubt and shame, demonstrating Erikson's (1959) psychosocial crisis of early childhood:
autonomy versus shame and doubt. Mahler and McDevitt (1980)
described the toddler's glee in the growing autonomy of the
practicing subphase, which is followed by the rapprochement-
subphase realization of his separateness and vulnerability and
threatened collapse of his self-esteem. To obviate this threat, the
mother must be emotionally available to the child and yet at the
same time must provide the child with a gentle push toward
independence. The analysis, not the mother, gave Casey the
"gentle push toward independence."

There was more interference from the parents than in the usual
analysis of a young adult. Casey's mother complained that she
was seeing too little of Casey, especially when Casey returned to

school for the basic education denied her because of her training for ballet. In addition, there was considerable resistance on Casey's part because she feared that exploring the maternal incest could mean that both she and her mother were homosexual.

Some months after she had begun to explore the sexual stimulation by her mother, Casey said plaintively, "It's one thing to say 'She did it to me' and I can be angry and hate her, but it's another to say I wanted it and went out for it. Did I feel I was to blame? . . . I still feel guilty." Still later she said, "She has a basic flaw, but if I give her up I won't have a mother." Casey had serious problems with college, for her conflicts over what she called "worries about what I am allowed to know" (about the relationship with her mother) intruded into most subjects, especially the humanities. For a long time she used her mother to quiz her, as if doing so would mean that her mother wanted her to learn. After quite a while, she studied with friends. As one might expect, her mother's sad retort was, "you don't need me anymore."

Casey's father was a successful professional tied to his career, glad that Casey's and her mother's preoccupation with each other made his wife less burdensome to him.

When Casey was in her mid-20s, she had a number of sexual relationships with men whose appearance, intellect, or personality problems were such that certain aspects of Casey's relationship with her mother were replicated all too easily. Casey could not reach orgasm. At the same time, the continuing influence of the mother's masturbation of her was demonstrated when Casey complained that she could not tell whether her body and genitals were being stimulated by her mother or her lover. She said plaintively, "Before, I could not get my mother out of my head. Now I can't get her out of my bed." Both foreplay and intromission caused anxiety because of this confusion.

She complained that her current lover, A, "used her," seemed to "turn on" to her and then to "turn off," much as her mother had. The analysis revealed that she had feared having an orgasm when masturbated by her mother, for having an orgasm would show her mother and herself that she enjoyed their sexual encounters. She had no orgasms with A. For about six months, material about A waned, presumably because Casey perceived that the relationship had no future. During this time there was a decided shift in the transference.

Casey now began to make demands of me in an entirely new way. Whereas earlier she had tried to coerce me to be a partner in the object-coercive doubting, her demands now were that I do what she wanted or that I not make her accede to what she felt was unfair. (These "unfair" demands were those that had been in operation throughout Casey's treatment and dealt mainly with keeping appointments, payment, and such.) Now she broke appointments without notice and announced that she would not pay for them. At the same time, she demanded extra appointments, telling me that she considered it her privilege to get them, even if it meant inconveniencing another patient or me. In contrast to the rather passive acquiescence she had displayed through the earlier phases of treatment, now there was more definiteness, more aggression in her demands, and, I felt, more of a sense of self. I found myself puzzled but not displeased by the change, and I sensed some amusement, which I understood when I envisioned her a foot-stamping two-year-old, demanding with a sense of justification that I not leave the city for a week of meetings because "I won't let you go away." "Why?" "Because I say so."

After a period of time, Casey again spoke of A, complaining that he used her and then ignored her. In spite of her complaints, her affect was such that I commented that she seemed not to want me to think that anything in the relationship had been of value to her or fun. Casey retorted, "You're too snoopy. It's none of your business." Although her voice was light, almost jesting, a quality she conveyed made me think that she was consciously withholding something.

She broke off with A after a painful argument. After a few lonely weeks, she met a new man, B, who was both more mature and more appropriate. She told me that sex with him was different from that with A. For several months, during sex with A she had had multiple orgasms from the time of intromission. With B, she had one orgasm with each intercourse, which they had many times a day.

I reviewed the recent material and commented that the "secrets'' about which Casey felt I was too snoopy had to do with her increased sexual freedom and her ability to have orgasms. I also noted that there had been a lessening and finally an absence of dreams about hairy spiders or octopi (which the analysis revealed to stem from the sexual exploitation by her mother). Casey was pleased to be capable of this sexual awakening and was especially delighted to have withheld from me the secret of her sexual fulfillment.

I interpreted this as meaning that her body, and her genitals in particular, belonged to her, not to her mother or to me. And her teasing about keeping the secret showed both of us that she had a mind of her own. I could see more clearly that the period in which she was negativistic and demanding, and yet secretive about her increasing possession of her genitals, had seen developmental strides. Whereas earlier Casey could ask (seldom demand) that she be treated as an exception because she had been sexually abused, now she conveyed "I deserve; I am entitled because I am separate, because I am I." She conveyed the pleasure of achieving a feeling of secure separateness never sufficiently experienced before. She now seemed to be fired by purpose and normal striving, not by humiliation. That Casey could be teasing and secretive, but had a growing sense of purpose, signaled that she was now handling her aggression more appropriately. Rather than being turned against herself, the aggression—now mixed with libido—was modulated, directed outward, and useful in helping her to proclaim ownership of her mind and body. The better sense of self, of knowing what was hers, and of possessing her own genitals were signs of progress, although at times they caused resistance in the analysis.

For the most part, the patient displayed aggression that was both hostile and nonhostile (Parens, 1973), but in both cases useful. Both forms of aggession had been severely compromised by conflicts caused by maternal incest. Now, I felt, the aggression subsumed in this special form of entitlement served to achieve, and even to enhance, the object representations that secured her from intrusion by the object, if only in fantasy, and from blurring of her ego boundaries.

The sense of entitlement, hitherto considered evidence of

pathology, may be considered to be a normal stage in the development of autonomy and independence of the body. Anna Freud (1965) suggested the possibility, although she did not designate it as such, as she depicted the overlapping and interrelating lines of development. If it is normal for children to demand because they have a sense of self and are struggling to achieve autonomy, can we not consider the entitlement that we see in some analyses to derive from the resumption of development?

Case #2

D, a 23-year-old, anxious, depressed woman, college educated but "going nowhere," was referred by her aging analyst when D took a job in Philadelphia. D hated to leave her former analyst, whom she regarded as handsome, charismatic, sorcererlike. She was angry at him because, although she knew that he was to retire soon because of failing health, she felt that he had encouraged her to move. She could not tolerate the dystonic thought that he might have wanted to rid himself of her and soon pushed the thought out of consciousness and concentrated on telling me of the many ways in which I was inferior to her former therapist. Her strong, positive, erotic paternal transference to him was obvious, yet for reasons she could not fathom she realized that she was relieved to be in treatment with me and not with him. She was extremely anxious and depressed. I felt that analytic psychotherapy, three times a week, with D sitting up, was the preferred form of treatment.

D was the third of five children, the only girl in a very chaotic family, with parents who prided themselves on being "modern." She felt that she was her father's favorite. Her father was the guru in a commune; they lived with many others in a rambling house with no doors on the bedrooms nor locks on the bathrooms. Sex talk was rampant; exposure to primal scene was frequent. There was considerable sex play in the attic/bedroom shared by all the children until D was 14 and the eldest boy was 18. As treatment proceeded, the picture of the family became more clear. D's mother seemed helpless to counter her husband's pronouncements on everything they did. She went along with his decisions on major and minor aspects of family living. Early in D's life, her mother—like her father—disregarded the needs of members of the family for privacy, regulation of aggression, establishment of appropriate behavior, and taking responsibility for school work. She obeyed her husband's firm and strange rules about health in general and about food in particular. Health was assured by limitations of food and complete freedom in sex.

When D, at age 9, well before prepuberty, complained to her parents of her brothers' sexual molestation of her, she was told to stop acting "like an old lady." When at 12 she told her father that a man on the commune had made sexual overtures to her, she was told that she had an overactive imagination. D's hyperacusis, which had always been obvious in the analysis, gradually took center stage, together with the frightening fantasy that my house was swaying. In spite of its solid construction, D felt that it might fall down. This ominous foreboding was seen in both transferential and extratransferential phenomena. Dreams and associations were to the emotional instability of life on a commune, with its many moves because of irate neighbors. At the same time, hyperacusis was associated to exposure to primal scenes, to fights between adults on the commune, and to excited listening to the approach of vigilante groups. Although both themes were obvious in her dreams and associations, the patient could not accept transference interpretations concerning her fear that treatment itself was unstable, that I, might "unload" her as her previous therapist had or that I would not protect her from the sexually attacking men. She said angrily, "You don't take me seriously." Her tone was like Chicken Little's predicting "The sky is falling!," although it conveyed anger rather than agitation.

During a tornadolike weather disturbance, she was troubled by the darkening sky, but especially by the noises of the increasing winds. She said, "Don't you hear the noise? How can you sit there?" I pointed out that her fear was occasioned by the noises but that old "inside" fears really caused her upset. At that point, a large limb crashed down from a neighbor's tree shattering the glass in a nearby room of my house. The patient gasped with alarm. Afraid that someone had been hurt, I excused myself and went to inspect the damage. When I returned, the patient seemed more relaxed in spite of the continuing storm. She smiled and said calmly, "This time you believed me." She could see that I had reacted and by doing so was verifying the truth in her experience. Instead of giving her "psychobabble," I confirmed her reality testing—she had been frightened by an outside threat, which related at first to her brothers', their friends', and her father's friend's molestation of her.

Soon material centered on her father. On coming to Philadelphia she had decided to take courses in a restaurant school in the hope of opening her own business. Courses on nutrition and food planning provoked a "learning block," for it was in those areas that her father's edicts had controlled the thinking and eating of the entire family. He had followed one dietary fad after another, from blackstrap molasses to all meat, to no meat, to high- and then to low-carbohydrate diets. At this point in treatment, D was certain that a single ice cream cone would cause hypoglycemia, a soda would cause stomach cancer, and liver should be eaten raw. The painful recognition of the oddness of her father's dietary pronouncements led her to face his other practices. He had paraded around the house nude to "let toxins be emitted through his pores." He had taught himself acupuncture and oriental massage techniques. She was afraid of needles and refused acupuncture, but she could not refuse the massage since it was "good for you." She also admitted, with shame and guilt, that she had enjoyed the treatments."

At this time D began to have an extreme aversion to her boyfriend's fondling her breasts during foreplay. She complained that I was not taking my proper role and that I should tell her to break off with her boyfriend "since he hurt me." I went first to earlier material about her brother and his friends tweaking her breasts, a painful-pleasurable experience. She was very definite, saying, "No, it's not my brother and his friends!" Soon she had dreams and fantasies of being in a zipped-up container that she could not leave. Then someone else was there, keeping her from leaving. She recalled sharing her father's sleeping bag on camping trips and the many massages he gave her. He would start on her back. She wished that I would scratch her "itchy places." Then there was a flustered, pained silence, after which she said, "I kept thinking of my breasts. It was nice, and it was awful." First she associated to nice times, then to awful times with her boyfriend; then she said flatly, "It's my father. He scratched my back and then went to my breasts. I know he massaged my thighs. I felt like screaming with excitement and pain. My mother should have forbidden it. I don't think she approved but no one could stop him, ever."

As D began to "dethrone" and demystify her father, she became able to learn and chose a career in law, a field her father hated!

Case #3

R was from a poor uneducated family but had performed brilliantly in school and at the urging of her teachers had attended college and pursued a graduate program in business administration. (Her mother's hope had been that R would become a telephone company operator.) R's superior intelligence enabled her to learn simply by listening to lectures and without having to study (i.e., to show her intention to learn). She had problems reading certain things; she could not tell time, read a road map or do simple "pencil and paper" arithmetic.

She came to treatment because of recurrent depression, low self-esteem, and great anxiety that occurred whenever, as a student advisor in a prestigious college, she was told by a student of having experienced incest. She was intelligent enough to know that these "reports" stirred something in her and was also well-enough informed to wonder why she had amnesia for the years throughout her prelatency and latency years until puberty.

During her sessions, R was troubled by a hypersensitivity to smell. She often thought that she detected a chemical smell in my waiting room or inner office; she disliked it and became anxious, although she could not say why. Later, when she associated the "chemical smell" to alcohol, she remembered that her parents had been alcoholics throughout much of her early life. After a "cure" through AA, her mother became hyperreligious and attended daily Mass. Like D, R was hypersensitive to being touched, to being carried (she was very petite and at times in their lovemaking her husband carried her to bed), and to her own touch of certain things. The reaction to touch and to being carried could be traced back to "some sort of molestation but by whom I do not know." Her revulsion to touching and to feeling recalled a hitherto repressed preadolescent fear of dogs, cats, and birds. She realized that she was not really afraid that they would bite her, but rather that she would "feel something solid, like a bone under the loose skin of the animal." She felt nauseated and accused me of making her experience feelings she did not want to experience, memories she should not be touching. She complained of the chemical smell again and said, "It's like the smell of semen."

I reconstructed that she was telling me of being touched, being carried against her will, and being made to touch (or to rub) something (a penis). I said she could recall the anxiety and revulsion and that she saw me, her therapist, both as the seductive male and as the indifferent female parent. The patient then remembered that when her mother was angry because her husband had abused her, she would make him sleep with one of the children and take the others to bed with her. He chose the child in a counting-down game that always ended with the selection of my patient. She had often puzzled about his way of "counting out." She knew now that he had fooled her with his numbers game and that in his gentler moods he was devoted and loving but, when drunk, had a fierce temper. R could not distinguish the noises of her parents' fighting from noises of their sexual activities. She began to remember hitherto repressed memories: of being carried to the "other bed," of being told to touch something, of not knowing whether he was the nice daddy or the fearsome one. At this point, she complained once more about the "alcohol-semen" smell, thus opening by this "somatic memory" memories of the sexual smells of incest with her father—alcohol and semen.

Case #4

Donald's analysis has been reported in detail elsewhere (Kramer, 1974). He had been referred at 10 years of age because of his "habits," that is, having to rise and sit down again a certain number of times in multiples of four. His parents requested an evaluation after he rose and sat 64 times in the midst of a raging summer storm; his mother worried what the neighbors might think! Donald was the only child born to parents who had married rather late. His mother was tied to her own mother; his father, to his own father. Donald's mother considered him strange looking from birth and felt that he was overly large, ugly, and too serious. His father spent a great deal of time with him, in part to protect him from the mother's carping.

Donald initially refused to come for treatment, and his parents complied with his wishes. Therefore, I did not see him until he was 15, when Donald and his parents were terrified by his mounting temper outbursts. At that time he came willingly, for he saw himself as a volcano that could erupt at any moment. He was extremely tall, cadaverously thin, and had severe pustular acne. He looked to the analysis as a place to get help with his temper, his separation fears, and his low self-esteem. Donald knew, but was afraid to acknowledge, that his mother was psychotic. In her interviews with me she revealed a paranoid psychosis. Donald complained about, but could not avoid, his extreme closeness to both parents. His father was his protection and yet stimulated Donald when they wrestled. His mother was "crazy-clean," yet she flitted into his room in ultra-sheer nighties, always using an excuse to intrude on him. Donald revealed that he had reached puberty early, having had his first nocturnal emission at $9\frac{1}{2}$. He had been plagued by sexual excitement, by obvious body changes, by the acne that his mother said was caused by his doing "bad things."

The analysis enabled him to face his mother's psychosis, to separate both emotionally and physically from both parents, and to live much as does the average teenager. He did well in school without needing to involve his parents. And he worked through the years of sexual excitement resulting from the fact that one or the other parent slept in his room from the time he was seven until he was 14; his excitement alternated with curiosity, as he listened at the wall between bedrooms, and with fury when he recognized primal noises from the adjoining room.

The "somatic memory" of maternal incest appeared during a period of severe regression near the end of his analysis when

Donald expressed the delusion that I could see his nose and lips get bigger and smaller, that I was refusing to tell him what I knew, but was instead keeping it to myself, smiling sarcastically. Donald was in great psychic pain and pleaded with me to "tell him the truth." We had long before analyzed his mother's and his own upward displacement from his genitals to his face; he had spoken of his anger at mother's perpetual, grimacelike smile, both sarcastic and seeming to "know" what others were thinking (and were saying about her, one of her psychotic mechanisms). After months during which he was agonized, sure that I knew but would not tell him of my awareness of his upward-displaced tumescence and detumescence, I made a reconstruction in which I said that I felt that something bad, indeed, happened; that someone had not only known but had caused the size of a part of his body—his penis—to change; that he was aware of that person's sarcasm. With surprise, Donald said "My mother bathed me until I was past 14. She bathed me all over." Donald found these baths to be exquisitely painful (emotionally), shameful, and exciting all at the same time. Since he reached puberty at 9½, he would become erect when she rubbed his penis. We were able to pursue the sexual abuse in the transference: I might have evil and magical qualities that enabled me almost to read his mind; he was able to agree with my assertion that he was sure that I could cause him to have an erection when we talked of sexual matters; finally he was able to acknowledge his pleasure in this fantasy as well as his exhibitionism when he implored me to look at him.

Williams (1987) said, "In reconstructing a seduction at an early age which led to a severe neurosis, no conscious recollections can be obtained" (p. 146). For Donald, the seduction had persisted until he was past 14. However, although he remembered being bathed, defenses against the entire gestalt included repression, displacement, denial, and projection. Williams referred to Freud (1918), who said that "[scenes that] further lay claim to such an extraordinary significance for the history of the case, are as a rule not reproduced as recollections, but have to be divined—reconstructed gradually and laboriously from an aggregate of indications . . . (p. 51).

I propose that in certain patients who have suffered childhood sexual abuse, the memory as such is not available or is only partially available. However "somatic memories" of the trauma persist and carry with them some of the actual sensation, fear, anxiety, anger, revulsion, and pleasure that accompanied the childhood seduction; concurrent with the "somatic memories" are learning problems, the nature of which may be specific for the particular child. In maternal incest, the learning problems are involved in pathological, object-coercive doubting.

Brenner (1988), studying sensory bridges to object loss during the Holocaust, said that some patients who suffered early object loss could conjure up memories of early sensory experiences that become bridges to the lost objects. I have found that sensory experiences in my patients provided bridges both to objects and to early experiences or to experiences too painful to integrate into the personality. At the same time I found that the learning problems were part of the process of repression that was used to deal with the painful and disorganizing memories of incest.

LEARNING PROBLEMS AND INCEST

There are many degrees and kinds of learning problems that arise in patients who did not experience incest. I have not, however, analyzed any case of incest that does not manifest some sort of learning difficulty. Several theoretical formulations are useful to explain this phenomenon.

The very title of Frank's (1969) paper on primal repression, "The Unrememberable and the Unforgettable," connotes the intrapsychic residues of early severe traumata. Frank says that even after secondary-process mentation has been firmly established, physiological, environmental, and emotional traumas may overwhelm the higher ego functions, and promoting regression, may create conditions suitable for passive primal repression. Although Frank's clinical material does not include incest, it involves late (adult) residues of profound infantile traumata. The analyst's reconstruction enabled the patient to "know," to "show that he knew," by questioning his parents about his having come close to freezing to death because of parental neglect. Frank feels that passive primal repression encompasses a developmental, rather than a defensive, vicissitude and that a common feature of passive primal repression is the absence of preconscious representation, which results from, among other causes, *mental overstimulation*. I am convinced that both physical and mental overstimulation may result in amnesia and in problems of learning. Just as in the case Frank cited, I feel that the memories of incest may be retrieved with the aid of reconstruction in psychoanalysis.

Woodbury (1966) describes defenses against intrusion by the incestuous parent that appears as a shell against both feelings and knowledge. He describes altered body-ego experiences similar to Donald's feelings that I knew what his body was experiencing (penile tumescence and detumescence displaced upward to his lips and nose). Donald was very certain of the changes in the size and firmness of his lips and nose.

Shengold (1967) described autohypnosis as a means of promoting isolation of affect "not only as a defense to deal with the erogenity and excitement involved in [his patient's] sexual wishes but also to bring about the repetitions of the post traumata in attenuation: the patient could do, with and to others what had been before done to her—now evading the overstimulation by way of hypnosis" (p. 407). Another patient he described (p. 410) had a general inability to integrate knowledge because of "the danger of re-experiencing the affects of the past" arising from the fact that he had shared his mother's bed from age three, when his father died, until past puberty.

He also reported a patient's use of massive isolation to "keep the overstimulation and rage in check." Shengold adds an important caveat, namely, that a special need for denial should alert the analyst not only to the possibility of psychotic or borderline ego, but also to the likelihood that he is "dealing with one of . . . the [people] who have lived through too much" (p. 414).

Elsewhere Shengold (1974, 1979) refers to "vertical splitting" a defense that makes "the good mother preservable only at the *expense of the compromise of reality testing by denial*" (pp. 107–108; italics added).

Repression may be partial, as in a case reported by Finkelhor (1979), whose patient did not forget that her father masturbated himself on her chest and later took her to the bathroom and had her soap his penis and masturbate him. She did not forget or deny the stimulation. Instead, she repressed her fury. However, when her fiance rubbed her breast she slapped him (pp. 185–214). She could acknowledge that her father's manual stimulation felt good, but that admission made her feel even worse, at the mercy of the adult, and out of control of her own body and emotions.

Others have reported on the interferences with thinking and learning in children who have been victims of incest. Ferenczi (1933) was very definite in his description of the child's inability both to know and to learn. He also alluded to the introjection of the *guilt feelings* of the adult. In describing patients with problems of doubting similar to those of my patients who had suffered maternal incest, he wrote,

> I obtained . . . new corroborative evidence for my supposition that the trauma, especially the sexual trauma, as the pathogenic factor cannot be valued highly enough. Even children of very respectable, sincerely puritanical families, fall victim to real violence or rape much more often than one had dared to suppose. It is the parents who try to find a substitute gratification in this pathological way for their frustration, or it is people thought to be trustworthy . . who misuse the ignorance and innocence of the child [p. 161].

He described interferences with the child's thinking and reality testing, as well as with his autonomy, and alluded to the formation of pathological defenses: "These children feel physically and morally helpless, their personalities are not sufficiently consolidated in order to be able to protest, *even if only in thought*, for the overpowering force and authority of the adult *makes them dumb and can rob them of their senses*" (p. 162; italics added). Ferenczi described identification with the sexual aggressor and went on to say:

> The most important change, produced in the mind of the child by the anxiety-fear-ridden identification with the adult parent, is the introjection of the guilt feelings of the adult which makes hitherto harmless play appear as a punishable offense.

When the child recovers from such an attack, he *feels enor-mously confused,* in fact, split—innocent and culpable at the same time—*and his confidence in the testimony of his own senses is broken.* . . . Not infrequently . . . the seducer becomes over-moralistic . . . [pp. 162–163; italics added].

The many mental mechanisms used to militate against remembering, against knowing, and against revealing what they have experienced has ruled incest victims' lives and colored their object relationships. The victims have low self-esteem, are self-critical, and have myriad doubts about themselves. It is for this reason that I feel (as does Shengold) that it is important that the analyst verify the incest experience as it emerges in treatment. I, for one, have never encountered an adult who has fabricated a story of incest. Most of them have had to repress, deny, isolate, or otherwise defend against knowing for psychic survival or for survival within the family.

SUMMARY

I have described two important residues of incest: (1) "somatic memories" and (2) problems in learning. In regard to the former, I feel that it is significant that incidents and affects that are otherwise repressed or denied persist in a somatic form. In discussing the related phenomenon of anniversary reactions, Dlin (1985) states that theories of childhood trauma and repression are important but are not enough to explain "the why," "the when it happens," and "why it takes the form it does." He characterizes the mechanisms involved as a trauma that is locked in or fixed, a "somatic time bomb waiting to be touched off by specific triggers" (p. 517). Such are the residues of incest that are activated by life events giving rise to the somatic memories reported by my patients.

The learning problems that I have described are a function, in part, of powerful resistances to remembering the events and feelings connected with the incest. Other contributing factors, especially in the young child, include identification with the abusing parent's distortion of reality and obeying the parental admonition not to know or tell of what has happened between them. In the older child, shame, guilt, and the need to deny sexual pleasure help to reinforce the not knowing. In children of any age, what begins as a defense against specific memories and their related feelings can become generalized into a cognitive style.

As a component of their learning problems, many incest victims demonstrate an inability to trust themselves to know or to trust others to be honest. This distrust has important technical implications for the analyst in helping these patients to reality test and therefore verify the actuality of the incest. (See Shengold, 1967, for a related view).

Sachs (1967) offered a relevant perspective when discussing the role of the analyst in helping patients to distinguish between fantasy and reality and their influences on conflicts, conflict resolution, and the behavioral residues of acting out. His description of what may happen when the patient is told by the analyst that some kind of trauma has, indeed, occurred is a poignant reminder of how meaningful psychoanalytic treatment can be for adult patients who were sexually abused as children. "There occurs . . . a release from obsessional self doubt which has affected some aspects of reality testing [and a strengthening of] the distinction of fantasy from actual events after their occurrence. . . . The belief and acceptance of the memory results in an exhilarating feeling of relief . . . at least someone believes me."

REFERENCES

Brenner, I. (1988), Multisensory bridges in response to object loss during the holocaust. *Psychol. Rev.*, 75:573–587.

Dlin, B. (1985), Psychobiology and treatment of anniversary reactions. *Psychosomat.*, 26 (6):505–520.

Erickson, E. H. (1959), *Identity and the Life Cycle.* New York: International Universities Press.

Ferenczi, S. (1933), Confusion of tongues between the adult and the child. In: *Final Contributions to the Problems and Methods of Psychoanalysis.* London: Hogarth Press, 1955, pp. 156–167.

Finkelhor, D. (1979), *Sexually Victimized Children.* New York: Free Press.

Frank, A. (1969), The unrememberable and the unforgettable. *The Psychoanalytic Study of the Child*, 24:68–77. New York: International Universities Press.

Freud, A. (1965), *Normality and Pathology in Childhood*. New York: International Universities Press.

Freud, S. (1918), Some character types met in psychoanalytic work. *Standard Edition*, 14:312–315. London: Hogarth Press, 1957.

Jacobson, E. (1959), The "exceptions." An elaboration of Freud's character studies. *The Psychoanalytic Study of the Child*, 14:135–154. New York: International Universities Press.

Katan, A. (1973), Children who were raped. *The Psychoanalytic Study of the Child*, 28:208. New Haven, CT: Yale University Press.

Kramer, S. (1974), Episodes of severe ego regression in the course of adolescent analysis. In: *The Analyst and the Adolescent at Work*, ed. M. Harley. New York: Quadrangle Press, pp. 190–231.

_____ (1980), Residues of split-object and split-self dichotomies in adolescence. In: *Rapprochement*, R. Lax, S. Bach, J. A. Burland, eds. New York: Aronson, pp. 417–438.

_____ (1985), Object-coercive doubting: A pathological defense response to maternal incest. In: *Defense and Resistance* ed. H. Blum New York: International Universities Press, pp. 325–351.

_____ (1987), A contribution to the concept "the exception" as a developmental phenomenon. *Child Abuse & Neglect*, 11:367–370.

Laufer, M. (1968), The body image, the function of masturbation and adolescence: Problems of ownership of the body. *The Psychoanalytic Study of the Child*, 23:114–137. New York: International Universities Press.

Mahler, M. S. & McDevitt, J. B. (1980), The separation-individuation process and identity formation. In: *The Course of Life*, Vol. 1, ed. S. I. Greenspan & G. Pollock. Adelphi, MD: U.S. Govt. Printing Off., pp. 395–406.

Margolis, M. (1977), A preliminary study of a case of consummated mother-son incest. *The Annual of Psychoanalysis*, 5:267–293. New York: International Universities Press.

_____ (1984), A case of mother-adolescent son incest. *Psychoanal. Quarterly*, 53:355–385.

Parens, H. (1973), Aggression: A reconsideration. *J. Amer. Psychoanal. Assn.*, 21:34–60.

Sachs, O. (1967), Distinction between fantasy and reality elements in memory and reconstruction. *Internat. J. Psycho-Anal.*, 48:416–423.

Shengold, L. (1967), The effects of overstimulation: Rate people. *Internat. J. Psycho-Anal.*, 48:403–415.

_____ (1974), The metaphor of the mirror. *J. Amer. Psychoan. Assn.*, 22:97–115.

_____ (1979), Child abuse and deprivation: Soul murder. *J. Amer. Psychoanal. Assn.*, 27:533–557.

_____ (1980), Some reflections on a case of mother/adolescent son incest. *Internat. J. Psycho-Anal.*, 61:461–476.

Silber, A. (1979), Childhood seduction, parental pathology and hysterical symptoms. *Internat. J. Psycho-Anal.*, 60:109–116.

Williams, M. (1987), After effects of early seduction. *J. Amer. Psychoanal. Assn.*, 35:145–165.

Woodbury, M. (1966), Altered body ego experiences. *J. Amer. Psychoanal. Assn.*, 14:273–303.

Issues
of
Technique

10 Psychoanalysis as Incestuous Repetition
Some Technical Considerations

Julien Bigras
(with the assistance of Karin Holland Biggs)

In 1897 Freud abandoned his theory of seduction and wrote to Wilhelm Fliess (Freud, 1892–1899) that he no longer believed in his "neurotica." He concluded that his patients' memories of childhood seduction were fantasies or purely imaginary inventions. However, like Ferenczi's (1933), my experience with incest victims has led me to revive the seduction theory, albeit with some modifications, in order to maintain the etiological function of incestuous trauma. In the brief space of this chapter I will discuss two hypotheses that support a modified seduction theory and the technical innovations they imply in the psychoanalytic psychotherapy or psychoanalysis of incest victims.

During the treatment of adolescent and adult female patients, I have found a sadomasochistic fixation on the abuser to be massively repeated in the transference with the male analyst. Furthermore, technical issues arising in the treatment of both groups of patients point toward two correlative factors in the

Editor's note: Sadly, Dr. Bigras died on June 13, 1989. This chapter as published here, may therefore not be in the definitive form he would have intended for it. I have chosen to include it because, even if not quite completed, it does reflect the ideas of an accomplished clinician who possessed an unusually extensive range of experience in the treatment of adolescent and adult victims of incest. As such, it stands as a tribute to his memory and a valuable contribution to this important area of clinical concern.

etiology of their severely disturbed object relations. Compounding the neurotic sequelae of incestuous trauma is an earlier, even more severe, trauma linked to maternal deprivation which I call "negative incest." Second, among more than half of the 14 adult victims of incest that I have seen as patients, the incest began in early childhood, at around the age of 2 or 3. Since this kind of information tends to be uncovered only after many years of analysis, it remains to be seen if "precocious" incest experiences will also be uncovered in the histories of the remaining adult patients in my care. Such revelations would not be surprising since incest reflects a problem within the family as a system. In such a family where severe disturbances exist not only in the relationship between the child's caretakers (the natural mother and father in the cases with which I am familiar), but intergenerationally as well, significant disturbances in the child's early object relations are to be expected.

Contrary to Freud's (1920) understanding of the transference neurosis as a struggle between a coherent ego and repressed traumas from childhood, the analysis of victims of incest must take into account the various splits in the personality and fragmentation of the ego (Ferenczi, 1933) that point to the need for narcissistic restoration and for a therapeutic alliance before interpretative work by the analyst will be accepted.

ADOLESCENT VICTIMS

In 1932, Ferenczi (1933) stated that childhood sexual trauma occurring at the hands of the parents could not be overvalued as a pathogenic factor. Incestuous seduction, he maintained, could provoke severe disorders, such as splitting of the personality, fragmentation of the ego, or even a state of atomization. My own experience over the last 25 years with adolescent female victims (Bigras, Bouchard, Coleman-Porter, and Tassé, 1966) and adult former victims of paternal abuse (Bigras, 1988) supports Ferenczi's views.

I have found that traumatic shock in adolescent victims is caused not only by the incest itself but by its eventual interruption. Over a period of 10 years in the 1960s, when I had in psychoanalytic psychotherapy 12 adolescent girls who had experienced prolonged incestuous contact with their fathers, a pattern was found to emerge in the circumstances and characteristics of what I came to call their "compulsive masochistic reaction" syndromes (Bigras et al., 1966) and in their transference behaviors to me. In each case, when the incest was revealed and the relationship with the abuser interrupted—for example, by the abuser's being jailed or thrown out of the home—the girl became overtly disorganized. Severe posttraumatic stress syndrome manifested itself in serious behavior disorders (running away, suicide attempts, depressive states, aggressive and opposition behaviors, sexual acting-out, drug addiction). In each of these 12 cases, I came to understand that the adolescent girl had been fixated submissively to her father from the first instance of the abuse. A tenaciously sadomasochistic couple had been established in which the girl submitted to the sexual and sadistic requests of the paternal partner even though, at times, she could also be aggressively provocative, even sadistic herself.

The disorganization entailed by the compulsive masochistic reaction can develop to the point of psychosis (which occurred in two out of 12 cases I treated). Driven by the repetition compulsion, the girl's promiscuous sexual activity enacts a search for a substitute sadistic partner; other acting out behaviors—drug taking, leaving home—are scenes in the drama of living out a destroyed object world, the paternal shield now absent. Acting out or psychosis is the only recourse open to the adolescent incest victim because she frequently cannot symbolize (in fantasy or symptom formation) her unstable or dead inner world. This sadomasochistic fixation, I have come to understand, serves to deny profound maternal deprivation. The loss of the abuser, sometimes the only member of the family with whom the girl has enjoyed some tenderness and degree of care, has left her unshielded before the full desolation of the mother-child relationship.

The compulsion to repeat the trauma, sometimes to the point of overwhelming both the adolescent girl and the therapist, constitutes the major transference process to be worked through.

The victims of incestuous fathers whom I have treated had profound sadomasochistic aims toward me from the very beginning of treatment.

One illustration of this recurrent phenomenon is the case of Manon, who was 16 when she began an 18-month psychoanalytic psychotherapy. At first we met twice a week and then increased our sessions to four times a week, after approximately four months, as soon as I found openings in my schedule. Before beginning treatment with me as an outpatient, she had been hospitalized after the latest of several suicide attempts. She had tried to commit suicide twice during several years of promiscuity following an overt and prolonged incestuous relationship with her father.

From the age of 10½ (when she menstruated for the first time) until she was 13, her father became aroused without warning on every contact with her. He bathed her himself; he caressed and masturbated her. She had to be compliant or else he became angry. She felt she could never relax around her father nor refuse his sexual advances. She kept their relationship a secret until her mother discovered it much later, and even then the break in the incestuous relationship was not due to any initiative on Manon's part.

Manon's mother was a more or less conscious accomplice to the incest. Even when mother "discovered" it, when Manon was 13, she suggested that Manon lead her father on so that he would be caught in the act. She wanted to produce evidence for the court and proposed that Manon should seduce her father and be caught naked with him in the bathroom by the police. Manon agreed to this, but then panicked when her father came into the bathroom. She quickly dressed and ran from the house. Her father was sent to prison, nevertheless, on other criminal charges.

During the period of the abuse, Manon drew no particular attention to herself at home or at school, where she was considered to be a very good student. Once her father was removed from the household, however, her behavior became disorganized. She began to steal and to act impulsively. In parks and streets she became the easy prey of men with whom she had sexual relations. Just as she had been unable to refuse her father, she was incapable of saying no to these invitations to brief seductions although she obtained no erotic pleasure from them. She ran away from home several times and made two suicide attempts.

With me, in psychoanalytic psychotherapy, Manon's behavior was extremely seductive and immodest, as it had been with other men she had known. She would allow her skirt to slip up to show her thighs, or she would walk around the office and deliberately stand close to my chair. She was masochistically provocative as well. She waited for me to order her to sit down again. She insisted that I control her. At times, she even wanted me to hit her, she said. Such behavior was often repeated in the early months of treatment. She flew into rages. She peppered me with direct questions, one of the most frequent being, "What do you think of me?"

Manon could not understand why I did not attempt to seduce her. For years she had been having brief affairs with men who "exploited and abused" her. They had always used her and had never shown her any gratitude or respect. She was completely at a loss, even angry, when I seemed to do nothing in the face of her invitations. "You've got something at the back of your mind," she told me. "You're laying a trap for me. It's not possible otherwise." She insisted on knowing my motives, "Why do you bother about me?"

My attempts at interpretation were refused, mocked, or met with a furious, obstinate silence. At other times they made her so angry she heaped ridicule on me and became destructive both in and outside the office. She managed to wear me down so effectively by insistent questioning, accusations, taunts, and complaints that I finally had to use a straightforward command—a direct call to order—to calm her down. The therapist who treats teenagers knows well that he is often called on to use some variation of the "call to order." This type of boundary setting is particularly necessary with adolescent incest victims because they cannot tolerate any frustration from the therapist, nor do they trust that he can control himself. The move by the therapist to impose limits in order to show respect for his patient and respect for himself is an early step in the process of forging, usually a very ambivalent alliance. In Manon's case, this inter-

vention, which was not experienced as a rebuke, seemed to
relieve her enormously.

Some time after this I left for a month's holiday. At the
resumption of our sessions, Manon's first remark took the form
of an aggressive question: "What good does it do you if I come
to see you?" Similar questions suggested that she was trying to
learn more about me, to test my trustworthiness. She seemed to
have gone beyond the uncontrollable fear that had fueled her
merciless provocations of earlier months. I interpreted that she
was wondering if she were important to me, if I were interested
in her, and if I could appreciate her. At this moment a dog began
to bark outside. She immediately said, "I dreamed about you. I
can't remember the dream, but it seems to me that I felt good."
She associated to dogs: "I don't like little dogs; I like big dogs—
watchdogs." She liked to imagine she had one with her wher-
ever she went.

Two striking incidents now followed that produced an important step forward in the therapy. They occurred about four or five
months after treatment had begun. First, Manon told me that for
the first time in her life she had, without hesitation, categori-
cally refused a man who had propositioned her in the park. She
told me this with great sadistic pleasure. "At last I succeeded in
making one of them pay; but they're all going to pay, the filthy
beasts (*salauds*)," she said.

At our next session I was inadvertently delayed and arrived
half an hour late to find that Manon had already left. The
following session brought a second telling development. She
explained that she had been extremely angry at being so severely
snubbed by me and was in a very bad mood. She remained silent
for several minutes and then said, "I'd like to dirty your walls
and wreck everything in here. I'm feeling sadistic." Then she
started to laugh like a small child who has lost control of a
situation—a loud, angry, explosive laugh that became a sob. She
said to me, "When I left here on Wednesday [the day of the
missed session], I was completely lost, I didn't know what to do
and I started to cry. I meant to run away. It isn't the first time, by
the way, that I've left home but I was sure my mother would put
the police on me. I hate the cops. Then I cried—I was furious. I

had an idea. You'll think I'm crazy. I went to the bathroom and pulled the curtains and locked the door. I sat on the floor in the dark for ages. After a while Mother knocked but I just stayed there, without moving.''

While telling me this, Manon mimed in front of me the position she had taken up in the bathroom. She sat on the floor, her legs a little apart, her elbows on her knees, her head in her hands. She suddenly blushed and said with embarrassment as she scrambled to her feet, "What'll you think of me?" I suggested to her that she had just understood what she was miming—a child on the toilet refusing to defecate.

Manon said that eventually her mother had shouted to her that she was going to fetch the landlord to open the bathroom door, so Manon decided to come out. Manon seemed to be proud of telling me that scene, as if she had defended herself not only against her mother but also against me. I interpreted she had asserted herself against the tyrannical parent's insisting she "produce" when put on the toilet. This self-protective behavior was all the more significant because in the preceding session she had told me about refusing the sexual advances of the man in the park. Perhaps for the first time she had put up an aggressive defense, both in word and gesture, against her analyst, who had humiliated her by not keeping an appointment. Following this episode, Manon defended herself much more frequently, particularly against her mother, who showed herself to be intolerant of this display of independence in her daughter. Treatment sessions became much more relaxed, to my great relief, as Manon seemed bolstered by greater self-respect.

The storm returned when I told her that in two months I would be going away for two weeks. Manon's reaction was violent. At the next session she arrived with an aggressive air about her and confronted me with a direct and challenging look. It was rather warm in the office, and she asked me to open the window wide (which was out of the question in view of the Siberian cold outside). She got up and belligerently yanked open the window herself. Then, approaching my chair, she said that she wanted to sit in my place, which was near the window, and told me to take hers. My look did not convey cooperation, and she furiously ordered me to do as I was told, saying that she was feeling sadistic and would like to hit me. Suddenly she jumped onto the back of my chair, making it rock back and forth. My first reaction was to get up in order to stop her, at which point she quickly sat down, looking very pleased with herself. She told me angrily, "I'd like to cut off your tie." At this point I had to intervene physically because she seemed to be on the verge of losing all control. I took her firmly by both wrists and led her back to her chair. Seeing that she had calmed down enough to listen to me, I interpreted to her that the wish to command, to occupy my chair, and to cut off my tie corresponded to her wish to possess me by force in revenge for having been misused by all the men she had known. It would also be a revengeful act of punishment for my plans to go away. This made her recall that, with both rage and pleasure, she had often imagined cleaving her father in two with an axe. She understood that it was to take this revenge that she wished to take the place of her father and make him suffer the fear, humiliation, and pain that she had endured.

At the next session she was pale and exhausted. Her eyes filled with tears as she flopped down into her chair. Since Friday, our last session, she had not been able to keep her food down and had slept fitfully. She had imagined having a big, friendly dog who would have kept her company over the lonely weekend. She remembered that when she was seven she had become attached to a little cat. She kept it with her constantly, snuggled in her arms. But the cat got lost, and she remembered feeling inconsolably sad and empty.

Since the last session she had not been to school and had vomited constantly. I noticed that she showed some of the signs, such as sunken eyes, of clinical dehydration. I emphasized to her that this state was an important message to me to look after her and not to retaliate for her attack on me.

She associated to this interpretation by saying that her mother just wanted to get rid of her and was not being supportive. "I should have been well rid of you if you'd succeeded in committing suicide," her mother often told her. At one point, her mother had even threatened to bring the father home again if Manon did not do as she was told. Manon started to cry, "No one has ever looked after me; I've never been a child. How much I'd like to be a child! I don't want to be an adult. I dreamed about you all the time, every night, since Friday. But it's all vague and I don't remember. I only remember one dream. You had to go away in February [the month of my holiday] and I would be left alone.''

These two sessions, in the context of my announcement of an impending absence, threw some light on the origin of this patient's deep narcissistic deficiency. She had a history of maternal neglect. Manon had never been able to feel at peace with her mother, who had never loved her. This child had spent much of her early years either with grandmothers or aunts or at boarding schools in the city where her family lived. Not until the age of seven did she spend much time with her mother in the family home.

Nevertheless, at this period of her treatment, these experiences were only hinted at by Manon. They did not yet form part of her associations, which constantly converged on memories of her father. I did not let go of this other guiding thread, but I did, from time to time, touch on the depth of her depression, which was founded on obvious maternal neglect.

After four or five months, when Manon's sessions were increased to four times weekly after my February absence, the therapy developed encouragingly. I noticed that she took more and more interest in serious reading and showed more curiosity and wonder about human emotions. I felt that Manon was showing a greater readiness to explore the unconscious.

She brought this dream one day: ''I came to see you in your office. At the end of our meeting, as I was leaving, the whole scene changed and there was nobody left in the world. There was nothing but wires, wires everywhere (the kind of wires used by tightrope walkers in the circus). I said to myself, I must go and find Dr. Bigras to explain this to me. Then a man appeared and said, 'You must walk on the tightrope for five days and then the earth will belong to you—you will have the world in your hands; you will rule the world'.'' Manon had this dream during that period in the analysis when she told me of her desire to make love to me. The dream suggests Manon would dominate the world if she had enough self-control to keep her balance on the tightrope for five days. In other words, if Manon could maintain a state of excitation and desire for a sufficiently long time without "taking action," she would control the world and be as strong as her analyst.

Her next dream was very painful for her to tell me. She had dreamed of an old man the night before. "I hate that old man!" she exclaimed. At this point, Manon looked at me intently and said, "Get away from me. I hate you." She became calmer again and told me the details of the dream: "The old man in the dream had claws like a tiger, and he scratched me until my thighs and legs and arms bled. He was very excited . . . a maniac. I'm ashamed because I didn't defend myself in the dream. On the contrary, I enjoyed it." Manon's face was contorted with anger. I interpreted that she was ashamed to tell me that she had enjoyed herself in the dream, just as at the beginning of the therapy she had enjoyed the thought of sexually provoking me. She told me that beating herself gave her great pleasure; it was not sexual pleasure but the "pleasure of rage." She asked me if this was masochism, and I replied that it was. "Why am I a masochist?" she asked, "For I am a sadist too. I'm sure I'm a sadist. But I'm just as much a masochist. When I was 11 I went through a very masochistic period. Every night when I went to bed, I took a cord and whipped myself on the thighs and arms and legs, and it was very exciting." Suddenly Manon remembered that it was at this time that her incestuous relationship with her father had begun.

The old man of the dream is her father, a violent and dangerous man. He is also the therapist, the man she desires. The masochism that appeared at the beginning of the incestuous relationship with her father may also be understood as an unceasing, compulsive repetition of the aggressive scene—the incestuous scene—during which she whipped up a feeling of rage and a wish for revenge.

Manon continued analytic psychotherapy for 18 months, in which time we reached her profound maternal deprivation. During that period I was to learn that Manon had also been precociously seduced by her father, who fondled her genitals when she was three and four years of age.

ADULT FORMER VICTIMS OF INCEST

In 1972, when I decided to restrict myself to private practice with adult patients, I continued to encounter, and to have referred to me, more and more female patients who had had incestuous relationships with their fathers during their childhood. Many of the adult victims I saw (at least 14 cases) came to analysis for reasons having nothing overtly to do with the incest experiences of their early years. Sometimes they were brought to me in a state of crisis but more often than not they came on a sudden impulse, having heard about or having read some of my writings.

At first sight the symptoms of these adult patients were much less serious than those of the adolescent girls I had treated earlier. In the adult group, the incestuous relationship had been stopped during adolescence, often at the initiative of the victim, without producing any massive, sudden disintegration. With most of those patients, symptoms manifested themselves not in behavior disturbances but in physical malfunctions related mostly to the genital area, although other organs or areas of the body were often affected. One patient was terrified by an auditory hallucination that consisted of sounds, quite soft at first, that became very loud and fast and then disappeared. Much later she associated these sounds to the spasmodic breathing of the abuser during orgasm. In another patient, there was a profound splitting of the ego. She told me that she had two bodies: one that carried on normally with the day's activities while another body floated in the air without managing to catch hold of the first one. After four years of analysis, another patient told me that she had recurrent dreams from which she woke during the night tortured by severe pains in the rectum and perineum. Those pains were so awful that she felt the need to put objects into her anus to calm herself. She was convinced that those pains were the equivalent of orgasms, and she would later associate them to incestuous activities to which she had been subjected from the age of two until she was eight, during which time the offender licked her genitals. This patient was also convinced that she was going to break down and become insane, in large part because of the "games" she was convinced I was playing with her. She believed that I was spying on her and calling her anonymously on the phone to insult her in French, a language she did not understand.

Little by little, these adult patients became able to disclose the serious problems that had marred their adolescence. These tended to be transitory problems of much less severity than those observed in the adolescent patients I treated but that, nevertheless, left irreversible damage: fragmenting of the family, erotic acting out of a masochistic type, impulsive and too precocious marriage or career choices, periods of depression with suicidal thoughts, depersonalisation phenomena, and, above all, low self-esteem.

Finally, it was through the relationship with me that the severity and depth of their suffering came out. They tolerated my absences only with enormous difficulty, and they were exceedingly vulnerable to frustration of any sort. Serious depressive episodes were frequent and sometimes were manifested in forms of physical and psychological collapse.

I believe the analyst is most tested when his patients relive the terrors that originate from the denial of their profound despair during the incestuous assaults. One patient related how, after an history of incest with her father, she had become attached to the leader of the gang with whom she hung out at the age of 14. Every night after dancing, she went to his room, where he lay her down on the floor, rubbed himself against her body, and threw her out afterwards. Only after three years of analysis did she suddenly understand that she had completely denied perceiving the erection and orgasm of her partner and most of all had denied the terror she experienced while being with him. It is therefore not surprising that this patient suffered from complete anaesthesia of the genital area.

An incest victim may be in therapy for years before posing the question of why she came to analysis. In many cases the terror associated with the idea of incest occurs in the transference, before the memory of actual childhood abuse can be uncovered. The case of Sarah, a successful professional in her mid-30s, well illustrates the kind of problems to be faced in the psychoanalysis of adult victims of precocious incest.

It was not until the sixth year of the analysis that the full details of Sarah's incestuous story came out. She had been repeatedly molested by a brother ten years older than she through violent oral and vaginal penetration from the age of two or three until the age of 10, when she was sent to boarding school. In her memories it was her father who had always sexually terrified her even though he overtly abused her only over a period of three years, from the age of 11 to 13. He used to drive her out to the country on weekends and stop the car in some hidden spot, where he would caress her genitals and masturbate himself. Sarah was as terrified by the sounds of his breathing, his "weird" look during the orgasm, as she was disgusted by the ejaculate spattered on her body, which made her vomit as it had when her brother had done the same to her. Images of the two men were condensed in her memory so that it was the horrifying face of the aroused father that haunted her.

During the first three years of analysis, Sarah spoke very little during our five sessions a week. She complained of nausea and cried a great deal of the time. She often felt chilled. Early in her analysis, Sarah experienced severe distortions of time in our sessions; she never knew whether we had only seconds, minutes, or three-quarters of an hour left. "What time is it?" she would ask all of a sudden. This disorientation, I believe, was due to her sense of experiencing the original trauma in the here and now in such an intense way that time seemed to have stopped. Furthermore, losing track of time was also a means of handing control over to me, making me into the abuser who alone had the power to release her from the torture of the sessions. I could not interpret these distortions at that time, however, since I did not yet know about the childhood and adolescent traumas even though I had some clues about her incestuous story.

Her maternal grandfather lived in the house during Sarah's early years. There was a kind of symbiotic relation between him and Sarah's mother. This relation was repeated between the mother and her son. Sarah and her father also formed a couple. As a child she always wanted to be with him and hated staying at home with her mother, whom she described as cold, distant, and verbally abusive. The father was an authoritarian, god-father type; he hated women and babies. He was aggressively critical of his daughters-in-law once they became mothers and held them responsible for the burden they and their children placed on their husbands. Everyone, including the sons, submitted to this behavior.

At the beginning of the analysis, Sarah could not tolerate my absences. For the first three years, she was so suicidal and unable to express her depression that she had to have at least one session a week during my holidays even when I was in a foreign country (where I would use a friend's office). Sarah had regressed to a state of total dependence to become even more "addicted" to me than to the males with whom she had been coupled throughout her life. As with other patients who were incest victims or who had narcissistic or borderline disorders, any change in our symbiotic relationship was experienced as intolerable.

It was in the fourth year of analysis that the incestuous nature of the transference became obvious. At that time, she had the dream of the "seesaw game." She told the dream to me expressly in terms of its being a sexual encounter between us. It reflected our profoundly sadomasochistic liaison. As the analysis progressed, this dream was remembered, recounted, and interpreted by her in different ways.

S: You and I were playing together on a seesaw on the sea. But the seesaw was shaped like a Cross, floating on its side. It rested on one end of the crossbar which acted like a base and a pivot for the seesaw-Cross. You and I were at opposite ends of the long horizontal beam. Although you were so much heavier than I, you were up in the air on the short end and I was half-submerged, clinging to the other slippery end with the pole pressing into my stomach. You've seen butterflies and spiders pinned in collectors' cases, haven't you? I felt like I was going to become one of those skewered specimens. You used the top of the crossbar like a lever to jerk the end of the beam I was holding on to up and down and sideways. You pushed it back and forth, driving my beam up and down, over and down, crashing me down into the sea, everywhere, never in the same spot, breathless. Each time you raised the bar, I surfaced choking and shivering, almost unconscious. You had absolute control over every movement of the seesaw. You thrust and swung and dropped me faster and faster, watching me become dizzy and more and more terrified. I thought, "Why is he being so cruel with me, so sadistic?'' Yet it wasn't really you doing it—it was as if you were being controlled by some invisible force. I knew the real you wanted to save me. You even had a plan. You stared into my eyes. You know, like you were putting thoughts into my head. "You mustn't let go of the beam. It could kill you with one blow," you seemed to be saying. You called directions out to me: I was to bring my feet up against the end of the beam and use it to spring backwards, almost like doing a backward dive. I managed to throw myself away from the beam, but after my backward leap I sank into the sea. You were watching me so I twisted to show you a message on my chest. It said "God" in red as if in neon letters or, perhaps, it was more like a brand right in my flesh. I thought I had been saved. At least, that's what I thought at the time.

This was the dream that had tormented Sarah during a period in the fourth year of analysis when she needed me so much that she thought of nothing else than for us to spend the rest of our lives together. She had bought a farm, somewhat like the one she knew I owned, in the hope that we could be together. She was ready to do anything to have me. This was the secret of her longing; it was a matter of life and death. And, in her dream, out of control, disoriented, and in pain, Sarah repeated this life-threatening, servile obedience, love, and fear she had experienced with a distant and authoritarian father, who, like a "godfather," seemed to hold her life or death in his hands (the word *God* had been branded into her own flesh). The dream expressed the violent self-destructiveness of the paternal transference, but it also signaled a turning point in our transferential relationship, as we will see later, from symbiosis, expressed in a sadomasochistic interaction, toward the expression of the maternal void underlying her sadomasochism (in the dream she sank into the sea, into death).

Confronted by her sexual dream, her mistrust, and her profoundly low self-esteem, I felt certain then that a real and violent incestuous relationship had occurred during her childhood. When I expressed such an interpretation for the dream, she confirmed it with the feeling that something horrible had happened to her as a child, but she was not able to name it. We do not know if it was at the age of two or three—Sarah does not remember exactly—but at the age when she was learning to speak she also had to learn to deal with sex and abasement. The adult males in her family (her father and big brother) played a direct role in the degradation she suffered, as did her mother, although in a different way.

The Double Denunciation

Shortly after telling me the "seesaw game" dream, and when she learned that I was to be out of town for two weeks, Sarah told me that she was thinking of committing suicide during my absence, "in an extremely gruesome way." It was the first time that she had expressed overtly suicidal thoughts. Nevertheless, this development seemed less dangerous to me than had the preceding three years, when I felt her to be much more depressed and suicidal even though she had never threatened to kill herself. Furthermore, while telling me of this thought, Sarah put more emphasis on the manner of committing suicide—in an "extremely gruesome" way—than on the finality of ending her life. I felt sufficiently reassured that she could tolerate my absence that I told her that I could not meet with her while I was away, nor could I leave my phone number (which was the truth, since I was going to be away sailing). She reacted with tears and feelings of a suffocating tightness in the chest and nausea. I then told her that I refused to be an accomplice to her "morbid thoughts" and that I could not change my plans.

On my return I was relieved to find her alive. Sarah had chosen between death and life and felt that for the first time she had control over her own life. In retrospect, her decision to live meant we were able to move beyond our sadomasochistic transferential liaison even though her physical complaints had become more severe in the interim. When I spoke to her during our first session on my return, she started and gave a shriek as if I had awakened her violently from a nightmare. Her abrupt scream surprised me so much that I jumped too.

B.: (firmly but gently) Why don't you tell me what's going on?
S.: (horrified) Your voice has changed. I don't recognize you.

She sounded as if she thought I was being deliberately cruel to her and repeated tearfully that her life had become an absolute nightmare during my absence. She had been overwhelmed by "destructive forces." She had been completely alone during my absence and knew she was at the end of her rope. This she told me in a reproachful tone of voice. As she started to cry silently again, I encouraged her a second time to speak to me.

S.: I don't recognize your voice.

She began complaining again of being a miserable mess.

B.: No, my voice has not changed with you. On the contrary, I am more on your side than ever. You feed these destructive forces in you even though they don't belong to you. They're like parasites, and I'm against them. I still refuse to be in league with them.

She then announced that she had had a nightmare that very morning, and I realized that my intervention had succeeded in calming her down a little. In the dream, she was in her father's car, and she could neither drive nor stop it even though she sat at the wheel. The car was making its own way in heavy traffic, zigzagging at full speed as if driven by a fugitive from the police. She was sure there was going to be a terrible crash. She woke up sweating.

B.: Here's the incestuous parasite that I'm talking about—your own father.

This dream, which was provoked by our separation, provided the opportune moment for the double denunciation: first of the incestuous crime and the "fugitive," the abusive father, and, second, of the absent analyst. Her own symbolic material incontrovertibly identified the fugitive as the one who controlled her psychic life and who was responsible for her behavioral disorganization. She was able to accept an interpretation explicitly linking her father to her fears, to her childhood abuse, and to the sense she had always had of being out of control.

The work of what I am calling the "double denunciation" is

significant for adult victims of incest at a number of levels. Time and experience have convinced me that it is the patient's profoundly low self-esteem that cannot be overcome by the usual working through of the analytic process. These patients not only feel profoundly guilty, ashamed, and worthless, but they are also convinced of having been so from the very beginning of their lives, in part because they were the blamed for having "provoked" their fathers to abuse, exploit, and humiliate them.

The double denunciation invokes realities that are both internal and external to the treatment. The first moment of the denunciation involves the expression of a reality judgment: the analyst recognizes and gives a name to that which had been nameless for the victim as a child—"incestuous abuse is a crime." Even when the child experienced some pleasure during the incest, the father's repetitive intrusiveness, his objectifying, mad gaze, and anguished breathing during orgasm ruptured the girl's sense of being and violently twisted her infantile sexuality toward an irreversibly masochistic expression.

In the second moment of the denunciation, the analyst is called upon to acknowledge openly that certain characteristics of the analysis will seem like repetitions of the original incestuous abuse: in an atmosphere of privacy the patient's intimate secrets are to be "exposed" and verbally "explored" with the male analyst. At the beginning of the treatment, this will be experienced as violent and violating by the incest victim, whose tenacious sadomasochistic defenses mask an even more extreme fear of exposure and intimacy. The analytic setting may not only reactivate the situation the child lived through with her parents—deprivation and loss of sense of being (Winnicott, 1965, 1971)—but also the shame of having no secret, private life as well. It is not an easy task for the analyst and the analysand to work this through. Moments in the incestuous transference will be as life threatening as were experiences with the abuser. Paradoxically, they will also be moments of great insight.

The double denunciation belongs to the process of repairing the narcissistic wound associated with having been treated as, and feeling herself to be, nothing but an object dirtied by use. In the "real" relationship in the analysis, through the denunciation, the male analyst enacts the role of a responsible figure who condemns as criminal the act of another male. He also acts as a potential new "father" figure who must prove he can be counted on to be consistently caring and dependable, trustworthy, and respectful. If the analyst should ever respond judgmentally to the patient as if he understood her to have made a sexual advance, then he will be repeating the same traumatic violation. By refusing the role of the sadistic paternal partner, the analyst becomes, in one sense, what Lacan calls "a representative of the Law" (Laplanche and Pontalis, 1973, p. 440). By reinstating the taboo of incest, the analyst begins the work of establishing the "Symbolic" (p. 439). Destroyed inner space begins to be knit together or overlaid with coordinates of time, of ethics, and eventually of desire. I am convinced that only after this move is made by the therapist can the primitive and archaic anxieties linked with maternal deprivation be worked though.

Negative Incest

A classical, silent, neutral analytic attitude can become unbearable not only for incest victims but also for suicidal borderlines and psychotics. These patients can experience the silent analyst as indifferent, rejecting, or absent. They reexperience the sense of nonbeing (Winnicott, 1971) that is at the core of their masochism and that they have already experienced in their early relationship to their mother. This is what I call "negative incest" (Bigras, 1988), a narcissistic vulnerability that is the empty legacy of the unavailability of the mother to her child in the earliest months and years, the preoedipal period. Her lack of profound care, of attentiveness, of desire for the child produces in the child an emptiness, a narcissistic wound, which is linked to death. It is in the gradual unfolding in the transference of the melancholic emptiness of the child for the missing mother, of the absence of desire, that the real work of the analysis begins and against which the sadomasochistic acting out of a defensive paternal transference has been the protective shield.

The denunciation not only has implications for developments in the therapeutic alliance, but it works to disrupt the patient's identification with the aggressor. The denunciation begins the process of uncovering the radical splitting that has occurred in all the psychical agencies of the incest victim. The earlier the abuse, the more serious the disintegration. The counterpart of introjection of the aggressor, through which the repetition compulsion operates, is the inability to symbolize the violence and terror to which the woman was subjected as a child, even before she could find proper words for the sensations she was experiencing. The child does not repress the violent events of her childhood but, far more pathologically, splits them off, losing not only the capacity to symbolize them but her desire, her memory, her sense of history as well. Moreover, what was "foreclosed" (Lacan, 1966) from the Symbolic reappears in the Real, as an hallucination or in the compulsion to repeat the trauma.

The absence of fantasy is at the center of negative incest (E. Bigras, 1988), and it is this lack that produces extreme and terrifying anxiety. Without desire, the victim of the maternal void (who may be any person suffering narcissistic fragility, not solely the incest victim) has only repetitive, uncreative dreams, if any at all; she lives in frozen time, criss-crossed with the repetitive patterns of relationships where she briefly finds a sense of self through the introjection of her sadistic partner.

For both Sarah and me, the seesaw game on the sea stood for intercourse between the father (me) and the little girl over whom he had total and abusive control. We wondered why in the incestuous act orgasm, as represented in the dream, could be reached only through death, that is, by going to the bottom of the sea (la mer) or by joining mother (la mère). Joining mother would then stand for Sarah's most secret (or morbid, as she called them) incestuous wishes. What had her mother to do with this?

I remembered that Sarah had once told me that it was not Mother whom she called Mama when she was a child, but her maternal grandfather, who lived with the family. I also knew that when she was frightened at night, Sarah would go to her grandfather's bed instead of to her parents'.

> **B.:** What did your grandmother do when you got into bed with her and your grandfather in the middle of the night?
> **S.:** My grandmother was dead.

B.: When did she die?

S.: She died the day Mother was born. My grandmother fell down two flights of stairs and died instantly, or so I was told. That's all I know. My grandfather never wanted to say anything more to me about it. After he died, no one would tell me what really happened to my grandmother the day Mother was born. All I knew was that Mother and her father were very, very close—they were inseparable.

I had the intuition that an important discovery had been made and I said to Sarah:

B.: The truth is that your grandmother killed herself the very day your mother was born. That is why, in your mother's mind, you are already a suicide, a child whose suicide is only temporarily postponed, as has always been the case for your mother as well.

That rang true to Sarah, who exclaimed that she had never understood why mother had never "belonged to the clan." Yet Sarah could not be certain whether the symbiotic relationship between her mother and grandfather had ever developed into an incestuous one. However, we could affirm that for Sarah, as for her mother, making love or giving birth to a child also meant killing oneself. This was the inevitable result of the fact that her primary link had not been made with the mother but had been established instead with the abusive father despite his sadism.

Over time we also came to understand Sarah's seesaw game dream as a wish to escape from the cycle of being carried away into brief, unfulfilling, and masochistic sexual encounters with men who were substitutes for the "Godfather." Most of all, in this particular narration of the seesaw game, we realized that Sarah had become more involved in her dream, able to relate it from her own perspective and able to speak in the first person singular, using expressions such as "I did . . ." or "I thought. . . ." She had begun to recognize her symbolic productions as her own "objects" and to feel relief and gain insight from our interpretations. The ability to symbolize and to make representations of herself emerged gradually in a therapeutic space where Sarah could have secrets and play without fear. It became a place where she felt "held" (Winnicott, 1971) and where she could mourn the mother who never held her. It became the place of escape from the infernal machine of the repetition compulsion into a place from which she jumped, somewhat tentatively, into new life experiences.

CONCLUSION

Many of the incest victims I have seen came to me with prior experiences with male therapists or psychoanalysts. Their complaints of being severely hurt and repelled by these attempts at therapy tended to fall into two types of failure. Either they had been sexually abused (and not only once in certain cases), which led to their leaving the treatment in crisis; or they had felt traumatized by encounters with cool and remote analysts. In both cases, they left treatment in a state of shame and despair.

When these women came to me I had to ask myself, Why have they chosen yet another male figure? I am tempted to answer that they felt compelled, once again, to go through the same sadomasochistic pattern. The working through of this compulsion could only begin, I soon realized, by the analyst's changing his attitude and manner of working so as to accept the importance of the real, as well as the transferential, relationship with this type of patient.

My experience with three male and four female analysts in supervision or in training analyses with me, when they were treating incest victims, has made it possible to formulate some as yet very propaedeutic observations with respect to the effect of the gender of the analyst on the treatment of female incest victims. The main difficulty male therapists encounter seems to be with their reactions to the seductive attitude and behavior of their female patients. If they are not overwhelmed (and so continue with incest victims as patients), then the next and much more serious countertransferential problem to be faced is linked to the profound oral deprivation of these patients. Tremendous work will be required of the analysts' own (self) analysis, and within their supervision, to find a way to be kind without being overprotective, present without being intrusive, available without being aloof.

With the four female analysts in supervision or analysis with me, we have determined that there is little danger of an erotic acting out either by the female incest victim or by the female analyst. Another problem, linked to a massive sadomasochistic maternal transference, can create real problems however. Over-compassion or overidentification with the girl's need to revenge herself against the abuser may produce too great a rapprochement between analyst and patient or its defensive counterpart, an extreme remoteness, which prevents a working through of the defenses against the despair accompanying negative incest. The requirement that the female analyst function as a representative of the law is as important as in the treatment conducted by male analysts; but the timing, transferential context, and form of the double denunciation by the female analyst, I believe, will differ from the constellation of factors appropriate to the male analyst's use of this move.

It is my opinion that both male and female analysts will have different but equally severe difficulties in working through the negative incest of the maternal transference. This pathology is one of the most intricate and severe that I have encountered in my career, almost as difficult as working with borderline and some psychotic patients.

Finally, the matter of ending the analysis of these patients deserves at least passing mention as it poses more than ordinary problems. Since the relationship with the incest victim is real and not solely transferential, a profound dependence on the analyst has been established that renders the ongoing analysis, and specifically its termination, particularly challenging. It is also to be expected as normal that in the months and years after the treatment has ended extra sessions will be asked for as our patients seek to protect the creative and caring relationship with the real person of the analyst that has been forged in the shared suffering required to go beyond the incestuous repetition.

REFERENCES

Bigras, E. (1988), Traitement psychoanalytique des victimes de l'inceste père-fille. Nervure, 2:64–65.

Bigras, J., Bouchard C., Coleman-Porter, N. & Tassé Y. (1966), En deçà et au-delà de l'inceste chez l'adolescente. *J. Can. Psychiat. Assn.*, 3:189–204.

Bigras, J. (1986), *La folie en face*. Paris: Laffont.

Bigras, J. (1988), Ce qui se joue dans l'inceste père-fille. Remarques sur la destruction d'une identité. *Nervure*, 2:54–64.

Freud, S. (1892–1899), Extracts from the Fliess papers. *Standard Edition*, 1:173–280. London: Hogarth Press, 1974.

_____ (1920), Beyond the pleasure principle. *Standard Edition*, 18:7–64. London: Hogarth Press, 1955.

Ferenczi, S. (1933), Confusion of tongues between the adult and the child. In: *Final Contributions to the Problems and Methods of Psycho-Analysis*. London: Hogarth Press, 1955, pp. 156–167.

Lacan, J. (1966), D'une question préliminaire à tout traitement possible de la psychose. *Ecrits*. Paris: Ed. du Seuil, pp. 531–583.

Laplanche, J. & Pontalis, J.-B. (1973), *The Language of Psycho-Analysis*, trans. D. Nicholson-Smith. London: Hogarth Press.

Winnicott, D. W. (1965), *The Maturational Processes and the Facilitating Environment*. London: Hogarth Press.

_____ (1971), *Playing and Reality*. London: Tavistock.

11 Clinical Issues in the Analysis of Adults Who Were Sexually Abused as Children

Howard B. Levine

Descriptive studies have proved invaluable in demonstrating the many long-term consequences of childhood sexual abuse (see Burland and Raskin, Steele both this volume). When applied in the therapeutic setting, they provide a set of presumptive indicators that can be used to raise a therapist's index of suspicion about the possible existence of repressed or suppressed childhood sexual traumata and their sequelae. The clinical merit of further such studies may, however, be limited. Accumulated data does not seem to support the definition of a specific syndrome that is unique to this group of patients. That this is so is not surprising. There is a tremendous variation in the nature and extent of the trauma, the gender of the participants, the relationship of the perpetrator to the victim, the age at which the abuse occurs, pre- and posttraumatic developments, including the nature and quality of the child's relations with his or her primary objects, and so on. What may prove more useful to psychoanalysts and other mental health practitioners at this stage in our understanding is an exploration of some of the clinical dilemmas that are likely to present in the analysis of patients who were sexually abused as children.

As the contributions to this volume document, patients who were sexually abused as children present psychoanalysts with a highly complex and difficult set of technical challenges. The treatments are frequently long and stormy, beset by prolonged periods of distrust and intense negative or erotic transferences. They are often characterized by strong tendencies to enactment and impulsive action and by such phenomena as primitive dissociative reactions, blurring of the boundaries between fantasy and reality, and reliance on archaic defense mechanisms, such as projection, projective identification, splitting, and denial, which are more usually associated with the treatment of borderline, narcissistic, and other primitive personality disorders. From a diagnostic perspective, it may be useful to think of many of these analysands as having a split-ego organization, in which a healthier, neurotic part of the personality alternates with or lies buried beneath a more impulsive, primitive part of the personality. This organization seems to be more pronounced when the childhood sexual abuse was violent or repeated or involved incest with an actual or surrogate parent figure. In this constellation, the primitive, trauma-related aspects of the personality may predominate for long periods of time, particularly when they become mobilized within the transference. They may then continue to exert their pressure on the analytic relationship until the conflicts and developmental disturbances to which the early sexual traumata have given rise are sufficiently worked through and corrected.

The clinical issues that have been raised in the preceding chapters and that I will elaborate on here do not occur either invariably or exclusively in the treatment of adults who were sexually abused as children. However, my own experience—which draws on discussions with the contributors to this volume; the cases presented by colleagues at the Workshop on the Analysis of Adults Who Were Sexually Abused as Children, held at the Boston Psychoanalytic Society and Institute from 1988–1990; and my own caseload—has shown that the issues I address here are encountered in some form in the majority of cases in which there is a history of parental incest or childhood sexual abuse.

THE QUALITY OF THE TRANSFERENCE AND THE ORGANIZING EFFECT OF THE TRAUMA

Despite the many complexities and difficulties involved, the cases reported in this volume demonstrate that adult patients who were sexually abused as children and who present within the framework of the widening scope of indications for psychoanalysis are more or less treatable by standard psychoanalytic procedures. That statement requires a bit of qualification, because one analyst's "standard" is often another's "parameter." Still, allowing for this heterogeneity in technical stance, it is safe to say that the analyses described in this volume are fairly characteristic of analyses as conducted in North America in this day and age and do not require any more divergence from the current norms of psychoanalytic technical practice than one is likely to find in any other group of treatments.

Given, then, that this is a representative group of a very difficult, hard-to-characterize, but more and more easily recognized set of patients, what might we say is characteristic of their treatments? Perhaps the most significant feature has to do with the quality and nature of the transferences that develop. For many of the patients studied, the actual childhood trauma tends to organize and unconsciously inform their experience of the analysis (and, indeed, virtually every relationship of any significance) and to dominate the transference for very long periods of time (see Williams, 1987). The quality of this experience often goes beyond the usual intensity of a transference neurosis. The pressure to reexperience and relive the sexual abuse can be enormous. It is not just that the transference is symbolically experienced or relived in relation to some derivative component of the childhood trauma. Rather, the compulsion to repeat is so powerful and the line between reality and fantasy so tenuously drawn that the transitional space in which the play of the transference neurosis usually unfolds frequently collapses. When it does, the "as if," illusory quality of the transference disappears (Levine, 1982). In the patient's psychic reality, *the experience of the analytic situation then becomes the trauma*, be it seduction or failure to protect. In this regard, the quality of the transferences that develop in the course of these cases, can, at times, be more akin to transference psychoses than to the usual neurotic transferences.

The unconscious organization of one's self, one's relationships and almost all of one's experience in the light of a single traumatic constellation and its sequelae is striking. The configurations that result are quite variable. Often, the consequences of this organization can be seen around boundary issues that arise either in the therapy—for example, in the handling of insurance payments or negotiations around hours—or in the patient's outside life. In the treatment of mental health professionals, these patterns may become manifest in the transference in the analysand's attempts to refer patients to the analyst or obtain clinical advice from the analyst about their own cases.

One problem that such situations present for the analyst is that maintaining the requisite stance of abstinence, neutrality, and analytic inquiry is at the expense of gratifying the patient's immediate wishes for help, collusion, and the like, and the analysand may respond to this deprivation with intense feelings of narcissistic injury. The analysand's response may represent the externalization of the patient's own harsh and critical superego, or the repetition in the transference of the analyst as unprotecting parent figure, or both. (See "Loss of Parental Protection" in this chapter.) Yet, to deviate from one's analytic position and attempt to deal with the issues raised at a "realistic" manifest content level—for example, accepting the referral or attempting to offer advice about how the analysand's cases might best be handled—may stimulate the analysand's fears of the analyst's corruption or seducibility.

This problem is complicated by the fact that deviations from an ideal of abstinence and neutrality occur in every analysis. They are the inevitable manifestations of the actualization of components of the transference neurosis and of countertransference-induced "failures" in the analyst's ability to maintain perfectly the purity of an analytic stance. When these deviations occur in the treatment of adults who were sexually abused as children, they offer ready opportunities for patients to experience the fear that they signal the beginning of an abusive transgression or narcissistic appropriation of one kind or another by the analyst. In more extreme moments, they may be felt by the patient as proof positive that a repetition of the sexual trauma or incestuous overture is literally and concretely in progress. Thus, for long periods of time, the analyst may be seen either as rejecting, devaluing, and not protecting the patient or else as taking advantage of the patient and using him or her for the analyst's own selfish, unconsciously narcissistic or erotized

needs. Being caught up in such complex transference developments requires continued self-analytic scrutiny by the analyst in
order to maintain the degrees of tact, sensitivity, and patience
that are necessary to help the analysand successfully negotiate,
recognize, and analytically explore the issues involved.

The enormity of the patient's internal pressure to repeat a
childhood seduction and to make the transference concrete and
real gives us some understanding of why patients who have a
history of childhood sexual abuse may be particularly at risk to
become sexually involved with their therapists (Smith, 1984). A
variation on this theme is for a patient with a history of
childhood sexual abuse to become involved with a charismatic
therapist, who may use the patient in a narcissistically appro-
priating, self-gratifying manner. While this exploitation may not
go so far as to include actual physical or sexual relations
between therapist and patient, the elements of transgression of
boundaries and symbolic reenactment of the trauma are evident.

No matter how great the pressure that a patient may feel
internally or attempt to mobilize in the analyst to reenact
literally the transgression of a childhood sexual trauma, *under
no circumstances is it appropriate for the analyst to offer direct
gratification of the patient's wishes for a symbolically or literally corrupt or physically gratifying relationship.* To do so not
only repeats the traumatic past, but constitutes a violation of the
patient's rights in the present and a breach of therapeutic ethics
and responsibility.

Any manifestations of the patient's experience, thoughts, or
emotional life may be drawn into the web of meanings related to
the childhood sexual trauma. When they are, it is as if the
unconscious fantasy life of these patients moves too readily from
preoccupation with the trauma and its derivatives to engross-
ment (see Myerson, 1969 for an elaboration of these concepts in
relation to the inner experience of the hysterical patient), and
then beyond that to a concrete, often unconscious conviction
that the trauma or its sequelae are being, or are about to be,
repeated and relived in the here-and-now immediacy of the
analytic relationship. (Recall from this volume Bernstein's
second patient, Mrs. L, who fled the session as the reality of a
childhood anal sexual assault was about to be reconstructed.) It

is the fluidity of associative connection and the regressive loss of boundaries between reality and fantasy that often accompanies it that give rise to many of the symptoms of sexual dysfunction from which these patients suffer (see Kramer, this volume) and to what the general psychiatric literature sometimes describes as "flashback experiences" in these patients.

A brief summary of two hours from the analysis of one patient, a woman in her mid-30s, who had been incestuously involved with both parents, may further illustrate these phenomena:

> The patient began the hour concerned about a relative's behavior at a family party. Elements of this behavior led associatively to memories of how, when the patient was between three and five years old, mother would use the patient's body to masturbate herself. Further thoughts led to pleasant memories of childhood visits to the rodeo with her family and her pleasure and excitement at watching the calf roping. Next, she thought of how "tied" she still was to her parents and her traumatic past, how both parents had tied her to them, greedily appropriating her childhood for their own sexual and narcissistic pleasure. The image of the calves with their legs tied up then gave way to father holding her hands and arms down as he molested her. As she talked, she became quite anxious and upset, and unconsciously assumed on the couch the posture she was describing—writhing, while holding her hands behind her over her head.
>
> In the next hour she was afraid to go further. She reported that following the previous hour, she had been terribly anxious and depressed all day. The memories of the incest had disorganized her thinking. She feared seducing the analyst or being seduced or taken advantage of by him. She worried that the material of the last hour, or this dialogue itself, might be the prelude to a seduction.

THE LOSS OF PARENTAL PROTECTION

It is not yet clear why the childhood sexual traumata of some patients exert this almost magnetlike effect and others do not. It is a phenomenon that I have observed in other, nonsexual, forms of early childhood trauma, such as early parent loss and, to a lesser extent, in the analysis of children of survivors of the Holocaust (Levine, 1982). I can only speculate about its meaning at this point, but it does seem related to situations where severe early childhood trauma is associated with the actual loss of parental protection. This feeling of loss may reflect the child's level of development at the time the trauma occurs, the nature of the early childhood, pretraumatic relationships and develop- ment, or some quality of the actual trauma itself. As I will describe the loss of parental protection, which is an important part of the basis for the "background of safety" (Sandler, 1960) in the analysis, seems to be an important component of how children experience incest and repeated or violent sexual abuse.

Alternatively, it may be true that any form of severe childhood trauma is accompanied by a premature and too sudden loss of the child's belief in the omnipotent protection of the internal- ized parent. This loss of protection often becomes connected in the patient's inner world with intense conflicts over abandon- ment and separation. In such instances, patients may appear to be quite masochistic. They struggle to hold on to a primary object representation, even if it is that of an abusing object, because of that object's importance to the organization of their self representations (see Valenstein, 1973). As noted by Steele (this volume), many victims of paternal incest suffer such pretraumatic deprivation in their mother–child relationship that the overtly incestuous object tie with father is their best—or only—source of comfort or warmth. This constellation of family dynamics may explain, in part, why some authors in the psychiatric literature (e.g., Yorukoglu and Kemph, 1966) have concluded that, in some patients, there were no long-term adverse effects of parental incest. In any event, that so many of these patients seem particularly vulnerable to feeling abandoned around times of separation and loss emphasizes the need for careful working through of these issues in the transference.

The loss of the parental protective function and its relation to conflicts involving abandonment and separation that have been found to be particularly prominent in cases of incest are worth further discussion. While almost all of the cases of incest presented in this volume reflect this phenomenon to some degree, Steele and Bigras (both this volume) are among the clearest in describing the betrayal of trust that is a crucial element in the trauma of parental incest. (Other traumatic components of incest include the problems produced by over-stimulation [Shengold, 1967, 1979] and the disturbance of the process by which the child moves away from narcissistic, identificatory relationships toward whole and separate object relationships with its primary objects [Loewald, 1979].)

The roots of the trust issue are complicated by the fact that parental incest is often built upon a preexisting state of relative maternal deprivation. That is, a maternally deprived child turns to father as a compensatory substitute for warmth, gratification, and protection. In many instances, such as the case presented by Huizenga (this volume), the father, too, feels deprived in his relationship to his wife and in his own early relation to his mother. The result is a father–child pair in which the prospect of closeness can too readily stimulate the intensification of mutually frustrated earlier needs. In such a pair, if these needs become erotized and the adult's controls are weakened by psychosis, alcoholism, psychopathy, impulsiveness, or the like, the danger of incestuous action becomes heightened. Then, should the incestuous breach occur, it may carry with it for the child the important intrapsychic meanings of the repetition of the loss of the protecting, nurturing mother and the loss or destruction of the father as a life-giving object and a substitute source of nurturance, protection, and attachment. With the relationship to a nurturing and protective object disrupted, the psychological background needed for play and fantasy, the protective envelope in which the playing child and adult must feel safely held, is destroyed and the act of play itself becomes libidinized through the incestuous violation. (See also the cases presented by Sherkow, this volume; and Galenson, submitted, cited in Levine, this volume).

The possibility of a preexisting maternal deprivation makes it difficult to separate the extent to which such findings as mistrust, fear of closeness, and difficulties in reality testing or in establishing a conviction about what one knows to be true are functions of the sexual trauma or are related to pretraumatic events within a disordered mother–infant relationship. The importance of this issue in the treatment of adults who as children were involved in parental incestuous relationships is, however, attested to by the fact that the exploration and affective reliving of the incest trauma often become engaged around the patient's experience of the analysis as a place of safety. The experience of safety in the analysis restores the lost parental protective function in which affects can be reexperienced and linked up to memories without danger of the recurrence of the trauma (see Huizenga, this volume).

THE DEVELOPMENT OF THE THERAPEUTIC ALLIANCE AND THE OPENING PHASE

The mode of organizing one's psyche around conflicts and derivatives of the childhood sexual trauma has enormous implications not only for the nature of the transference that unfolds, but for the difficulties encountered in the development of a therapeutic alliance as well. As Raphling (this volume) has described, and I have repeatedly observed in other cases, these patients are liable to demonstrate a resistance to the formation of a therapeutic alliance. This resistance is partly based on the intense pressure to repeat or reexperience the trauma that arises whenever a close relationship is at hand.

Patients cannot trust themselves or their analysts not to engage in illicit—symbolic, or actual—traumatic repetitions of the childhood trauma. The distinctions between fantasy and reality, past and present, remembering and reliving, are either threatened or lost. Adult, cooperative parts of the patient's ego, including the capacities for self-observation and the formation of a therapeutic split, are often overwhelmed by the intrusion of powerful negative or erotic transferences. Thus, it is not unusual for some patients who are aware of having been sexually abused as children to resist the recommendation for an analysis for long periods of time.

Patients who do begin analysis may avoid mentioning or affectively engaging in the exploration of these memories until the beginning-phase issues of trust and safety have been firmly established in their minds. Their reticence may delay or disrupt the successful transition from psychotherapy to analysis or prolong the opening phase of an analysis for a considerable time. In some cases, the dynamic determinants for the patient's decision to reveal the sexual trauma and begin to explore it seem to be related to a combination of the development of trust in the analyst and the activation of issues of loss and abandonment in the transference (see Huizenga, this volume). This latter finding is of particular interest in the light of the loss of parental protection that the child may have experienced as a part of the trauma.

The formulation of a therapeutic alliance not only necessitates the patient's emotional investment in and recognition of the presence of another object, with all of the dangers of injury, seduction, and betrayal that that entails, it also ultimately requires an acknowledgment of previously unacceptable sexual and angry feelings and the relinquishing of characteristic defensive stances against these, such as entitlement, projection, blaming the abusers, and clinging to a self-definition as victim. It is not unusual for patients who were sexually abused children to hold to a relationship to the analyst that is marked by a defensive counterdependency and self-sufficiency for very long periods of time.

An interesting variant of this position is the patient's adoption of a "self-analytic" stance, in which the interpretations of the analyst are never taken in directly during the session. Rather, they are listened to, stored, and then considered or applied by the patient outside of the analytic hours, away from the bodily presence of the analyst. A careful exploration of this phenomenon with one patient revealed that it was an attempt to maintain control over the analytic relationship, benefit from anything good that I might have to offer by way of interpretation, and still protect herself from the influence and control of my potentially overwhelming or seductive intrusions.

Another impediment to the development of a therapeutic alliance is the patient's defensive reliance on a self-defined role as "victim." The analysis of this position must be handled with particular sensitivity. The sexually traumatized child *was* victimized by the adult. And in today's society, there is enormous cultural support for viewing adults who were sexually abused as children only as victims. In attempting to explore the defensive uses to which a patient may be trying to put the childhood sexual abuse in the current treatment, an analyst must be sensitive to these cultural forces and take care not to fall into the stereotyped role of blaming the victim.

From a *moral* point of view, I believe that in the adult–child relationship the burden of restraint clearly lies with the adult, whose responsibility it is to care for and protect the child. In this sense, these patients were the victims of their seducers. At the same time, from an *analytic* point of view, we must not lose sight of either the defensive uses to which a patient may put the victim status or the wishful components that may have been unconscious motivational factors in the childhood sexual encounter (see Greenacre, 1950). In addition, the usual oedipal and preoedipal longings for sexual and physical gratification may become condensed and associated with memories of the trauma in a process of retrospective elaboration in fantasy, as the child attempts to explain why the trauma occurred. This is a normal component of the child's posttraumatic adjustment process: the attempt to deal with and detoxify the impact of the sexual trauma by fantasy elaboration of memories of the actual events. The result, by the time the child presents as an adult, may be a characterological picture of extreme guilt and constriction.

Organizing oneself around the victim role may also limit the scope of what is available for self-observation and therefore for analysis. In many instances, early childhood seductions become the basis, by way of identification with the aggressor, for later seductive behavior in early adolescence or adulthood (see Bigras, Steele, this volume). For example, one patient who had been sexually abused by both parents in early childhood and latency reported that during adolescence she sought out her father for sexual contact and attempted to seduce other older male acquaintances. While the reconstruction and understanding of these events was leavened by the recognition of the role played by the earlier seductions and her identification with her aggressors, it would have been a serious omission not to address the guilt that followed from her subsequent active sexual provocations or to consider her only to be a "victim" or "survivor" of incest.

ASSERTIVENESS, DESIRE, AND THE SENSE OF OWNING ONE'S BODY

The definition of self as victim can also have important conse-quences for a patient's attitude toward his or her activity, assertiveness, adult responsibility, and desire. Ehrenberg (1987) noted that incestuous and sexually abusive relationships in childhood can have a "profound impact on the nature of the [adult] individual's patterns of relation to desire" in both a sexual and a more general sense. "Without minimizing the traumatic nature of the actual violation of the child, which is intrinsic to the incestuous relationship" Ehrenberg attempted to demonstrate that *one of the most devastating aspects of sexual abuse,*

> *and the one most usually dissociated or denied by [the victim], is the fact of the victim's own active participation and responsive-ness in these relationships. . . .*
>
> To the degree that arousal of the victim's own desire is experienced as the basis for the vulnerability [to the incest], the relation to desire becomes quite problematic. This is particularly so when the relationships in question endured over considerable periods of time. In such instances it is clear that unless the child had been a cooperative participant, and derived some gratifica-tion from the involvement, the relationship could not have been possible. The individual's coming to terms with his or her own participation in these early relationships, . . . constitutes one of the pivotal issues in treatment. [pp. 593–594, italics added].

Needless to say, these are issues that can be taken up only with the greatest tact and care, after the basis for the protective security of the analytic relationship has been carefully estab-lished.

Another issue that is closely related to the disavowal of desire and that must often be addressed in the analysis of patients who were sexually abused in childhood is a damaged psychological sense of owning one's body. Prior to puberty, a child's body representation is not yet fully vested as belonging to the self. A residue of infantile symbiosis remains in the unconscious attitude that the body still belongs to the parents. It is only after the developmental tasks of early adolescence are consolidated that children begin to feel fully in possession of their own bodies. The process of developing a proprietary sense of one's own body seems particularly vulnerable to disruption if the child is chronically subjected to traumatic relationships with primary objects who narcissistically appropriate the child or its body for their own use. Thus, this problem is especially likely to be present in patients who were incestuously involved with a parent.

For example, Kramer's (this volume) patient, Casey, demonstrated her developing sense of self possession by keeping from her analyst her new-found genital sensations and sexual fulfillment. In another patient, anger and negativism, which had served other purposes for long periods of time earlier in the treatment, reached a point where they were predominantly being mobilized in the service of asserting control over her own body. Slowly and painfully, her analyst learned the importance of recognizing and interpreting the developmentally progressive component of her anger as it appeared in the transference. Interpreting it as a resistance, as evidence of a frustrated wish or in any other way that implied it was *only* pathological or ought to be given up, felt to this patient at this time in her treatment like another appropriation or exploitation of her body by the analyst/parent. Subsequent to the recognition and working through of this issue, this patient was able to assert her own control over many things, including the time and place of sexual relations with her fiance. At first, this newly asserted attempt to control her bodily self made her feel guilty. She feared hurting her fiance or provoking him to angry, retaliatory action. Issues relating to penis envy and fears of castrating wishes emerged simultaneously and were addressed. But what seemed unique and significant to this phase of the treatment was the interpretation of the patient's wish for and response to her newly developed sense of ownership of her body and sexual response.

DOUBTING AND THE WISH TO KNOW

When patients who suffered childhood sexual abuse do relate memories of the abuse experience, it is often with a great deal of doubt and uncertainty about what actually happened. This may be as true for those analysands who enter treatment aware that a sexual trauma took place in childhood as it is for those whose memories of the abuse emerge from repression or are reconstructed during the course of treatment. The intensity of the doubting may surprise an unsuspecting analyst, especially when the patient is dealing with memories rather than attempts at reconstruction and these memories date from a time in childhood when an analysand would be expected to have a clear sense of whether the memory was real or fantasy. Kramer (1983) described one aspect of this problem as "object-coercive doubting" and related it to maternal incest. I have found it to be a more extensive phenomenon that occurs in almost every case of parental incest, regardless of the sex of the parent involved. It may even evolve into a global cognitive style that leads to generalized difficulties in learning (Bernstein, Kramer, this volume).

At some point in the treatment, the doubting and uncertainty about "What really happened?" "Was it real or fantasy?" may assume center stage for the patient and produce difficult technical challenges for the analyst. Patients may beseech the analyst to offer them help, certainty, or confirmation in knowing what took place or demand that the analyst express belief in their doubt ridden accounts. At one level, this phenomenon may represent a transference repetition. That is, the patient is asking, Will you recognize and identify for/with me what is really going on as I wished my parents or other significant adults to do? Or will you turn away and pretend not to notice or even covertly foster the continuation of the incest as my parents did?

Simultaneously, the doubting may unconsciously repeat the trauma. That is, the patient, in the unconscious role of the incestuous parent, may be angrily or seductively attempting to make the analyst do something to relieve the patient's distress. Or the angry doubting and cranky demands may reenact feelings of undischarged sexual tension, which were an important part of

the abuse experience (Shengold, 1967). In relation to the analyst's proper role in the treatment, the elements of narcissistic
use of the object and the demand for transgression of boundaries
inherent in this transaction are readily apparent to the observer.
These meanings are apt to be much less apparent for the patient,
however. The result is often some of the most complex and
difficult moments in the analysis. Regression, a weakened
alliance, hypersensitivity, and confusion, on the part of the
patient can run headlong into the analyst's countertransference
strain. The latter arises from the analyst's perception that the
patient is attempting to force him or her to take sides, to know
omnisciently what was or was not real, or otherwise to abandon
a position of abstinence, neutrality, and an optimum analytic
stance.

In trying to find one's way through this complex and demanding set of problems, an analyst must assess the extent to
which some active support for the patient's reality testing is
necessary or possible. For very young children, it is the parent
who helps define what is "real" or proper. This fact of development has obvious implications for future reality testing in
cases of parental incest. In addition, many patients did not have
in childhood adequately protective or reality-supporting objects
who would affirm that the seduction of children was wrong and
not the fault of the child or to whom they could "report" their
abusive parents. For many children, the limitations of the
parents were compounded by their own guilt by threats made
and enticements not to tell. One patient reported that her father,
with whom she had an incestuous sexual relationship for many
years would say about many things, "A person is always free to
choose what they want." The contribution in such pronouncements to later doubting and confusion about what is real is
apparent.

Clearly, then, some patients, in this moment in the analysis
seek to enact the wish that the analyst function in a longed for,
but never provided, protective, parental role. But what are the
consequences of the analyst's attempting to satisfy this need for
the patient? Will doing so prove helpful, or will it unconsciously
reenact some component of the sexual trauma? Will it foster
regression by attempting to fulfill a universal childhood longing

for an omniscient object? Will it encourage a sense of entitlement to be compensated for the sexual trauma, or will it
reinforce the patients' views of themselves as victims and
thereby contribute to their suppression of either fears or perceptions of their assertive or seductive behaviors?

These are difficult questions, and their answers must be
determined individually in each instance. At issue is the analyst's assessment of how much the patient is able to bear the
existential burden of not knowing and accept the necessary
uncertainty that surrounds almost any "truth" that derives from
the subjective realm of psychic reality. For the analyst, the
technical dilemma that this produces is bounded, on one hand,
by what Bigras (this volume) calls "the double denunciation,"
that is, the "law giving" call to order, "This was wrong!" On
the other hand, there are the questions of whether such a stance
will further resistance and whether an analyst can ever really
know what happened. As Sherkow (this volume) says, the best
that we may be able to do is reconstruct what is "likely" rather
than what was "true."

From the point of view of the analyst, as long as the patient is
deemed to be analyzable, the issue of whether or not one can
"know" what was or was not real may be moot, especially in
regard to technique. One does not have to decide for oneself
whether something was actually real or not. One only has to
recognize and acknowledge the tremendous importance that the
wish for certainty holds for the patient, analyze the fact and
consequences of the patient's uncertainty and doubting, examine the ways in which doubting the experience may have
been reinforced by the child's own guilt and by the action of the
parents, explore the meanings that the doubting assumes and the
uses to which it is put in the transference, and try to follow the
evolution of the material within the analytic process.

THE EXPERIENCE OF THE ANALYST

Thus far, my discussion has focused predominantly on the
patient's experience in the treatment. No examination of the
analytic clinical process would be complete, however, without

giving thought to the experience of the analyst. As Bird (1972), McLaughlin (1981), and many other authors have stated, the often painful and disruptive emotional engagement of the analyst in the analysand's transference neurosis is an essential and inevitable component of the treatment process. What can we say about this aspect of analytic experience in the analysis of adults who were sexually abused as children?

Lisman-Pieczanski (this volume) offers us a starting point in her candid description of the emotional turmoil produced by her attempts to analyze her patient, S. At different junctures of the analysis, she experienced curiosity, confusion, "deadness, irritation, outrage, and hopelessness," a sense of losing her bearings, or fear that she was violating the rules and risking rejection by her "analytic parents" for breaking the law. In accordance with the dominant transference paradigm of the abused and violated child, and the patient's rapid unconscious oscillation between the role of abused and abuser in the transference, Lisman-Pieczanski also felt sadistically cruel, afraid that her patient was dying, and the sense of being a helpless and abused infant herself, assaulted by feelings of impotence and rage.

The list of the analyst's likely affective reactions to becoming immersed in a treatment in which childhood sexual abuse and failure of the parental protective function are constantly being relived and repeated could be extended. One could include affects of excitement, disgust, outrage, voyeuristic fascination, wishes to protect or repair and all of the reversals, defensive vicissitudes and responses to these. In fact, many of these are implied or mentioned in passing in the case material of the preceding chapters. There is one particular countertransference problem, however, that deserves further elaboration because it has not yet been sufficiently appreciated as a vicissitude of the treatment of adults who were sexually abused as children. That is the analyst's response to his or her own feelings of boredom, affective deadness, confusion, and unrelatedness.

These affects may exist for very long periods of time in the analysis as a consequence of the patient's counterdependent needs to maintain a radically self-sufficient stance. This stance can lead the patient to an intense withdrawal from emotional contact with the analyst and produce in the analyst profoundly disruptive feelings of emotional deadness, confusion, intense isolation, and despair. The motivational impetus for this process is unconsciously determined by the patient's desperate wish to maintain control of his or her physical and emotional boundaries; to avoid dependency, closeness, and the longings that these inevitably produce; and to protect against the desires for and fears of the repetition and reenactment of the infantile sexual trauma. In addition, the deadness may also reflect the patient's or the analyst's defenses against his or her own desire, the patient's inability to trust in the reliability and safety of the object, the dissociated and withdrawn affective state of the overstimulated child at the moment of the trauma, the lost and depressed child of the posttraumatic period, the depressed relationship with the unavailable early mother, or the damage done to the patient's symbolizing capacity (see Huizenga, this volume). The disturbance in symbolizing capacity can severely constrict the ability of the patient's ego to represent elements of the trauma and its aftermath or to forge affective associative connections between these experiences and other sectors of the mind. Whatever the underlying dynamic causes may be in any individual case, the result is that the analyst must be prepared to immerse himself or herself in an ungratifying situation of affective deadness for long periods, until the underlying meanings and conflicts that support this massive affective withdrawal are understood, analyzed, and worked through.

THE PRESENTATION OF CASE MATERIAL

A final note related to countertransference issues and the ways in which childhood sexual traumata may be symbolically enacted or felt by the patient to be actually repeated in the treatment concerns the analyst's writing or presenting of psychoanalytic papers. In a broad sense, a major component of the repetition of the childhood sexual trauma revolves around the question of unauthorized appropriation of that which is the patient's for the gratification of others. To whom does the analytic case material belong?

Aside from two recent articles by Stein (1988a,b) that touch upon the subject, the psychoanalytic literature pertaining to the ethical dilemmas of presenting clinical material is quite sparse. Our traditions, going back to Freud, place considerable emphasis on case reporting as a means of instruction and communication. Current concerns about the analytic process require ever more complete descriptions of clinical material. In an attempt to foster a more informed scientific discourse, our reports must be sufficiently intimate and detailed to allow the reader to generate alternative hypotheses about the material presented and to provide critics of one position or another access to data that would allow them to refute the propositions being offered by the author.

From what I have been able to gather anecdotally, the standard of practice of psychoanalytic writers regarding patient consent is quite variable. Everyone would take care to disguise the material presented, so that patient confidentiality was protected and the identity of the analysand could not be determined by the reader. But what of the patient identifying his or her own case in the writings of the analyst? Or the matters of ethics that reach beyond those of patient identification? Some analysts obtain permission from their patients before any case material is used. Others do not. Some even go so far as to show the patient the proposed clinical writeup, so that the patient has an opportunity to give truly informed consent for its use. There is, at present, no uniform practice regarding these matters in our field.

In the course of preparing this book, I have had many conversations with colleagues and contributors about the question of content. These conversations have made me aware of the many ethical concerns about scientific publications and presentations that had been unrecognized, dormant, or too lightly regarded in the wake of my own authorial ambitions and desires to communicate with colleagues. Although all authors are free to follow the practice that feels most comfortable and consistent with their role and responsbilities as clinical psychoanalysts, I have personally come to believe that this area deserves far more careful scrutiny by our profession than it has so far received.

For adults who were sexually abused as children, the unauthorized use of clinical material may represent the repetition of the trauma of misappropriation. Although writing or delivering a psychoanalytic paper is clearly not the same as the sexual seduction of a child, no matter how nobly intended the scientific purposes of the communication may be in the mind of the analyst/author, it may very well repeat the violation of the seduction in the mind of the patient. Thus, contributions have gone unwritten and illustrative vignettes omitted, because the analyst felt that the treatment was not yet at a place where the analysand could be presented with the analyst's desire to use some portion of the material for his or her own ends, albeit scientific and professional ones. Or analysands have not given consent for material to be used—even when they acknowledged that the material was unobjectionable, respectful, and accurate— on the grounds that to allow the analyst to do so would still feel too much like another violation.

To my great personal relief, I have found that whenever a patient was presented with the request for permission to use some portion of the case material for scientific purposes, the impact on the clinical process was salutary, even when the permission sought was not granted. To be sure, this outcome reflected the fact that the decision to risk such an intrusion into the analytic process had been carefully thought through by the treating analyst, well-timed, and handled with tact and respect. Such concrete evidence of the analyst's sensitivity to the patient's needs and wishes, interest in the patient's problems, and willingness to cede the ultimate decision to the patient had a powerful impact on the patient's view of the analytic relationship. It helped further differentiate the patient's image of the analyst from abusive figures in the patient's past and the regressive transferences that they determined. For some analysands, the analyst's request also provided an opportunity for further reworking of material related to the sexual abuse, as it rekindled, albeit in a contained and controllable way, residual elements of the trauma in the transference.

I hope that our current social climate of increasing awareness and willingness to recognize the pathogenic importance of childhood sexual abuse will make it progressively easier for material of the sort presented here to emerge before the public eye of scientific discussion; that analyst/authors will become ever more sensitized to the value and necessity of truly informed consent; and that analysands will feel increasingly more comfortable in allowing us the proper use of what is a jointly owned body of material, the analytic data. In the meantime, I feel confident in speaking for my colleagues and contributors as well as for myself, when I offer the hope that this volume will continue to stimulate a vital and constructive dialogue that will lead in turn to greater therapeutic effectiveness in dealing with the consequences of childhood sexual abuse and incest.

REFERENCES

Bird, B. (1972), Notes on transference: Universal phenomenon and hardest part of analysis. *J. Amer. Psychoanal. Assn.*, 34:275–288.

Ehrenberg, D. B. (1987), Abuse and desire: a case of father–daughter incest. *Contemp. Psychoanal.*, 23:593–604.

Greenacre, P. (1950), The prepuberty trauma in girls. *Psychoanal. Quart.*, 19:298–317.

Kramer, S. (1983), Object-coercive doubting: A pathological defensive response to maternal incest. *J. Amer. Psychoanal. Assn.*, Suppl., 31:325–351.

Levine, H. (1982), Toward a psychoanalytic understanding of children of survivors of the Holocaust. *Psychoanal. Quart.*, 51:70–92.

Loewald, H. W. (1979), The waning of the Oedipus complex. *J. Amer. Psychoanal. Assn.*, 27:751–776.

McLaughlin, J. (1981), Transference, psychic reality and countertransference. *Psychoanal. Quart.*, 50:639–664.

Myerson, P. G. (1969), The hysteric's experience in psychoanalysis. *Internat. J. Psycho-Anal.*, 50:373–384.

Sandler, J. (1960), The background of safety. *Internat. J. Psycho-Anal.*, 41:352–356.

Shengold, L. (1967), The effects of overstimulation: rat people. *Internat. J. Psycho-Anal.*, 48:403–415.

_____ (1979), Child abuse and deprivation: Soul murder. *J. Amer. Psychoanal. Assn.*, 27:533–559.

Smith, S. (1984), The sexually abused patient and the abusing therapist: A study in sadomasochistic relationships. *Psychoanal. Psychol.*, 1:89–98.

Stein, M. H. (1988a), Writing about psychoanalysis: I. Analysts who write and those who do not. *J. Amer. Psychoanal. Assn.*, 36:105–124.

_____ (1988b), Writing about psychoanalysis: II. Analysts who write, patients who read. *J. Amer. Psychoanal. Assn.*, 36:393–408.

Valenstein, A. (1973), On attachment to painful feelings and the negative therapeutic reaction. *The Psychoanalytic Study of the Child,* 28:305–392. New Haven, CT: Yale University Press.

Williams, M. (1987), Reconstruction of an early seduction and its aftereffects. *J. Amer. Psychoanal. Assn.,* 35:145–163.

Yorukoglu, A. & Kemph, J. P. (1966), *J. Child Psychiat.,* 5:111–124.

Author Index

Subject Index